NO PROBLEMS HERE?

Keith Carby was born and educated in Derbyshire. Although he took a first degree in chemistry he later read for a higher degree in research methodology in the social sciences. He then joined the staff of the late Dr Nicolas Malleson to take charge of research in a special unit based at the University of London. The unit, which was funded by the Department of Education and Science, was involved at the national level in investigating and assisting in the redeployment of 'discontinuers' from higher education.

He has previously published the results of research work in the natural sciences and is author of the IPM publications,
Transactional Analysis at Work
Job Redesign in Practice

Among recent publications by Manab Thakur, published by the IPM are:
OD: the Search for Identity
Manpower Planning in Action
Testing People at Work
Performance Appraisal in Perspective

NO PROBLEMS HERE?

Management and the multi-racial workforce including a guide to the Race Relations Act 1976

Keith Carby
Manab Thakur

Institute of Personnel Management
Central House, Upper Woburn Place
London WC1H 0HX

Published by the IPM 1977
and produced in cooperation with
the Commission for Racial Equality

© Institute of Personnel Management 1977

All rights reserved
No part of this publication may be reproduced, stored in a retrieval system, or transmitted in any form or by any means, electronic, mechanical or photocopying, recording or otherwise without written permission

Film set by David Green (Printers) Ltd and
printed in Great Britain by Butler and Tanner Ltd

ISBN 085292 151 9

Contents

Acknowledgements

The authors are deeply indebted to all those organizations and managers who have contributed information for this publication. We are also especially grateful to Dr Alan Little and Susan Sengupta (CRC) for their invaluable assistance. Many other people have freely given assistance and thanks are particularly due to F C Hayes (Training Services Agency), David Lane (CRE), Mary Coussey (formerly of the Race Relations Board), David Smith (Political and Economic Planning), Dr Michael Pearn (Runnymede Trust), John Brock (London Business School), Karamjit Singh (Leicester CRC), Tom Jupp (National Centre for Industrial Language Training), David Chakravarti (Birmingham CRC), Ukwe Ejionye (CRC), Dr Peter Sanders (Race Relations Board) and Harold Bird (Department of Employment).

Foreword—No problems here?

I welcome this comprehensive assessment of race relations in employment, drawn from studies of a selection of companies with differing needs and practices. It appears at a particularly relevant stage of the development of equal opportunities for ethnic minority groups in this country.

Equal opportunity and non-discrimination in employment have been recognized for many years as central to the whole issue of fair treatment for minority groups, and this emphasis on employment is reflected in the new Race Relations Act which includes stronger investigatory powers against discrimination and which widens the definition of discrimination to include discrimination in effect. The Commission for Racial Equality, which has just begun its work, will pay particular attention to the development of equal opportunity in employment; in addition to carrying out investigations where discrimination is believed to take place, it will offer encouragement and advice to employers wishing to develop positive policies. One of its major tasks will be the drawing up of a Code of Practice on the employment of ethnic minority groups, which will provide guidance to employers on what needs to be done. The conclusions drawn in this Report, and the findings of the study of race relations in employment on which the Report is based, will make an important contribution to our preparatory work on this Code of Practice.

The Institute of Personnel Management is to be commended for its work on this study, which was carried out with the support and active cooperation of one of our predecessors, the Community Relations Commission. In addition to discussing the findings of the study of employment practices, the book provides a useful summary of the new legislation and background information on ethnic minority employees. I hope its publication will stimulate personnel managers and everyone responsible for employment decisions to take positive action by reviewing their procedures and practices and ensuring that they are free of discrimination. For the good of the whole nation, we must make equal opportunity not just an aspiration but a reality.

David Lane

Chairman, Commission for Racial Equality

Introduction

All races

This book is intended to be an aid to managers and others having an interest in organizations which employ multi-racial work forces. Its main purposes are to assist managers who want to improve the effectiveness of their organizations through the elimination of racial discrimination and disadvantage, and to help organizations comply with the Race Relations Act 1976.

A great proportion of workforces could be said to be multi-racial in nature and the issue of eliminating racial discrimination and disadvantage is not confined to those organizations situated in areas with high immigrant populations. The underlying principle of the 1976 Act is equality of opportunity *for all* regardless of race, colour, nationality or ethnic or national origins. To limit anyone's chances in life purely for reasons of race is equally repugnant whether the victims be white or black, British or foreign. There is little doubt that, at present, the problem is most acute among members of racial minority groups and in particular for black members of the community. Consequently, although in principle all that is written applies to discrimination against all racial groups, our attention is primarily focused on people of Asian, African and West Indian origin. (The term 'racial minority' and the word 'black' are used throughout. These are not synonymous but where appropriate they are often used to refer to the same groups of people. Neither term is regarded satisfactory but they are used in the absence of any acceptable but brief alternative). For similar reasons, our interest is largely concentrated on the less skilled in the labour market.

The study

At the time of writing, the Royal Assent had been given to the Race Relations Act 1976 but the introduction of the law was waiting for the new Commission for Racial Equality to become operational. As it was clear from the Bill that this proposed new piece of legislation would have significant implications for employing organizations and their managers, the Institute of Personnel Management wanted to assist its members and other managers to comply with the letter and the spirit of the law. Because of the generous support and invaluable advice offered by the Community Relations Commission (a forerunner of the Commission for Racial Equality) the IPM was able to set up a study into the management of multi-racial work forces so that the implications of the new law could be seen in a practical context. This study was in no way intended to reveal the extent of discrimination and it was not meant to be a highly systematic piece of research. The idea was to seek out the common managerial difficulties that were currently reputed to arise as a result of employing members of racial minority groups. We especially wanted to discuss these problems with managers (principally managers but also trade union representatives, black employees, white employees and people well versed in race relations in employment), and to consider options that existed for coping with them particularly in view of the provisions of the 1976 Act.

The study was undertaken in three stages. First, most of the agencies and notable individuals in the field of race relations in employment were consulted and asked about key issues. Secondly, visits were made to 22 organizations employing multi-racial workforces. These organizations, which were situated in either Birmingham, Manchester or South London, were selected so as to give a reasonable coverage of race, the proportion of racial minority groups in the workforce, the type of industry and so on. The sample was therefore not claimed to be representative of employment as a whole but was designed to provide practical examples of problems typically said to arise in the management of multi-racial workforces. The contacts in the main were personnel managers but on most occasions a wide range of members of organizations were included in the discussions at some stage.

The final stage of the study was the convening of a one day working seminar for managers and others well versed in race relations and employment. Some of the major issues arising out of the visits were discussed in detail at the seminar.

Issues old and new

The information gathered throughout the study was used as the basis for this book. Some of the issues covered are claimed by some to be virtually 'problems of the past.' This refers to the more obvious difficulties associated with large-scale immigration such as vast cultural and language differences. There are those who contend that it would be better to concentrate almost exclusively on the emerging problems of restricted opportunities for young black Britons who differ significantly from their contemporaries only in their racial origins.

In the event we decided to include these so-called 'old problems' principally because our visits to organizations showed that they are still very much in evidence. Also, although the form of these problems may differ, they essentially result from the same phenomena, racial discrimination and disadvantage.

Contents

Part I of this book provides various arguments in favour of managers taking steps to eliminate racial discrimination and disadvantage. The case is argued from the point of view of organizational effectiveness as we believe that, in today's society, tolerating racial discrimination carries penalties which impair organizational performance.

Some notes on the Race Relations Act 1976 are provided in Part II. These should help managers to understand the major features of this legislation.

Part III looks at specific aspects of employment and racial minorities. A checklist of questions to be used in an initial diagnosis of the need for action is given and information on policies, affirmative action and record-keeping is also included. Finally, four appendices are added: Some further statistics on racial minorities, The background of Asian minority groups, Some notes on relevant agencies and advisory bodies and A short reading list.

PART I
THE CASE FOR ACTION

Fact not fiction

In taking any initiative, managers in the modern enterprise will need to bear in mind the attitudes and beliefs of their managerial colleagues, trade union representatives and employees in general. Efficient management will also assess how closely these views match the facts. A careful examination of both attitudes and objective data is especially necessary in race relations because of the existence of a highly distorted but pervasive racial mythology. In particular, there are many popular misconceptions about the presence of black people in organizations and in our society at large. The following data should help organizations separate fact from fiction as a first step in considering the case for action.

Immigration, education, social services and housing

The following are some factual responses to a few of the more widely held racial 'myths' on immigration, education, social services and housing.[1] *

Immigration

FICTION *There is uncontrolled immigration into this country*

* All numbered references are listed on page 155.

FACT This is not so. Under the Immigration Act 1971, very few categories of people can come and settle in this country. They are:

Commonwealth citizens, whose parents or grandparents were born here

Spouses/fiancé(e)s and specified dependants of those already here

Certain people with UK passports who have no other citizenship

All European Economic Community nationals have the right to work in any EEC country. The member states of the EEC are Britain, France, West Germany, Italy, Denmark, Belgium, Holland, Ireland and Luxembourg.

FICTION *Immigration is making us an overcrowded island*

FACT Since 1964 more people have left the UK each year than have entered. In 1975, 190,000 people came to live in Britain and 230,000 left, a net loss of 40,000. (Office of Population Censuses and Surveys.) The population of the UK fell between mid-1974 and mid-1975. (OPCS.) Holland, Belgium and West Germany, all prosperous industrial countries, have more people per square mile than the UK. (Pan World Atlas, 1973)

FICTION *White people are leaving this country and are being replaced by black immigrants*

FACT Only one in every three immigrants to this country was born in the New Commonwealth; this includes all the present Commonwealth except Australia, Canada and New Zealand. (This also includes Pakistan which is not a member of the Commonwealth.) (Census 1971.) The countries of birth of people who came to the UK between 1971 and 1973 for at least a year and were not born here were as follows:

41 per cent New Commonwealth
15 per cent Old Commonwealth*
44 per cent Other (OPCS)

FICTION *The numbers of births to black immigrants is increasing all the time*

FACT The number of births to mothers born in the New Commonwealth fell from 46,100 in 1970 to 39,000 in 1975. (OPCS)

FICTION *There are large numbers of illegal immigrants entering the country*

FACT It is impossible for anyone to know how many illegal immigrants there are, but some indications can be drawn from the figures below:

In 1975 only 188 people were detained and removed as illegal immigrants

In April 1974, the Home Secretary announced an amnesty for certain illegal immigrants; after two years only 1,990 people had applied. (*Hansard*, Commons, Col 580, 24 6 76)

FICTION *The Home Office is concealing the facts*

FACT The Government publishes the facts about immigrants in the following ways:

The Census (1971 is the latest)
Home Office Immigration Statistics

*Officially, the members of the Old Commonwealth are Australia, Canada and New Zealand. The New Commonwealth consists of the relevant African nations, India, Bangladesh, Cyprus, Malta, Gibraltar, Malaysia, West Indies and several other countries. Pakistan is not a member of the Commonwealth but figures for Pakistan are often listed along with statistics for the New Commonwealth.

Department of Education and Science statistics on numbers of immigrant pupils
Department of Employment counts of unemployed people
Registrar General's returns of births and the International Passenger Survey
The General Household Survey of the Office of Population, Censuses and Surveys
Answers to Parliamentary questions (*Hansard*) (Her Majesty's Stationery Office)

Education

FICTION *Because they don't speak English they hold back our children at school*

FACT Many children of immigrant parents were born here and English is their first language
Most local education authorities make arrangements to teach English to non-English speaking children in special classes with special teachers so that they do not impede the progress of the rest of the children. (*Immigrant Pupils in England*, National Foundation for Educational Research, 1971.) There is no evidence to say that the proportion of black children in a class has any significant influence on the attainment of white pupils. (*Language Proficiency in the Multi-Racial Junior School:* A Comparative Study, NFER, 1975; *Race and Education across Cultures,* Heinemann, 1975)

Social services

FICTION *Blacks come here to sponge off the state*

FACT Blacks as a group are younger than whites, so proportionately more blacks than whites are working and therefore paying income tax and national insurance; 91 per cent of black men are working compared with 77 per cent of white men. (*The Facts of Racial Disadvantage*, Political and Economic Planning, 1976.) Since there are proportionately fewer older people in the black community, they take much less from the state than the white population. Black people are likely to receive only 80-90 per cent as much as their fellow citizens from state funds for health, welfare, education, social services and housing. (*The Economic Impact of Immigration*, Cambridge University Press, 1970)

Housing

FICTION *They get priority in housing*

FACT Four per cent of Asians and 26 per cent of West Indians live in council house accommodation, compared with about 30 per cent of the population as a whole. (*The Facts of Racial Disadvantage*, PEP, 1976)

FICTION *Immigrants are running down our inner-city areas*

FACT Urban decay has existed in this country since the Industrial Revolution. Bad housing conditions were here long before black immigrants. In the areas where 70 per cent of black people live, eight out of 10 people are white. (Census, 1971)

Number of immigrants

According to the 1971 Census, just under three million people living in Britain were born overseas. Of these,

1.15 million came from the New Commonwealth; 0.7 million from Ireland; nearly 1 million from European and other similarly developed countries; and 0.14 million from the Old Commonwealth. In fact, therefore, two out of three people born overseas but living in Britain were white. The latest available figure for the number of people of New Commonwealth and Pakistan origins given in mid-1975 (Social Trends No 7, 1976) is 1.8 million, which represents 3.3 per cent of the total population of Great Britain. There is bound to be a small rise in this proportion over the next two decades as the black population tends to be younger than the rest of the community.

Employment

Most of these black people came here in the 1950s and 1960s when the United Kingdom, like most other European countries, was very short of labour. In certain cases, workers from New Commonwealth countries were asked directly to come here and contribute to the country's economic growth. As one Report[2] on *Western Europe's Migrant Workers* puts it:

> The plentiful supply of relatively undemanding labour, young and hardworking, has favoured a degree of economic development that would not have been possible without it. They have increased productivity by removing labour bottlenecks and have encouraged capital investment by being more prepared to work night shifts. They have kept wage levels from rising too fast, and at the same time have enabled European workers to move into higher skilled jobs. They have been less demanding on the social services because of their age structure, and have been prepared because of their mobility to move in and out of short-lived jobs.

Undoubtedly these migrant workers and their countries of origin have also benefited in the process but this does not in any way diminish the contribution they have made to the economic growth of the United Kingdom and of most other European countries.

It is estimated that around 7.5 per cent of the total British labour force is made up of migrant workers. The corresponding figure for West Germany and for France is roughly 11 per cent and for Switzerland around 28 per cent.[3] Such comparative data do not seem to prevent some people claiming that immigration should be stopped and even that 'repatriation' schemes should be set in motion. The recent high level of unemployment has been used to strengthen these arguments since it is often taken for granted that 'immigrants come here and take our jobs'. As most immigrant workers came to Britain when there was a clear demand for their services this belief is well wide of the mark in terms of the history of immigration. Nowadays, immigrants still tend to be found in low-grade, low-status jobs and in kinds of work that many white workers would prefer to avoid, no matter what the level of unemployment. It should also be remembered that it is hard for overseas workers to get permission to work in this country. Work permits are not issued to people from the New Commonwealth or anywhere else if the job in question can be filled by a local person. In 1975, 2,074 year-long work permit holders from the New Commonwealth and Pakistan were admitted to this country. Another 7,986 came in from other non-EEC countries including the Old Commonwealth.[4]

Born in Great Britain

Some further data on racial minorities are given in Appendix 1 but perhaps the most striking statistic concerning black people in Britain is the number born here. According to the 1974 estimates, 40 per cent of black people in the population were born in Great Britain. We therefore already have a large proportion of black people for whom limited opportunity cannot so easily be blamed on their recent arrival from another country, their 'foreign' origin, or their refusal to give up a completely 'alien' way of life. Some black youngsters may have spent their lives in a particular sub-culture but the same is true for white children brought up in a Glasgow tenement or on a Suffolk farm.

Discrimination and disadvantage

Organizations which employ workers from racial minority groups and are free from discriminatory practices appear to be rare indeed. The existence of deprecatory racial myths of the kind already listed is just one indication that racial prejudice clearly exists in the rest of our society, so it would be surprising if this social malignancy had not found its way into the world of work. There is evidence, however, to suggest that the past performance of employing organizations in ridding themselves of racial discrimination has been disappointingly poor.

> Difficulties with regard to employment, often directly related to discrimination or prejudice, are the most widespread single source of disappointment with life in Britain for coloured immigrants. The discrimination they face individually or collectively in employment is the factor most frequently mentioned to explain why they think some kind of colour bar exists in Britain today.[5]

Evidence of racial discrimination in employment

During the last 10 years, several research studies have proved the reality of racial discrimination in employment. One of the most comprehensive studies,[6] which looked at discrimination in key areas throughout society, was done before the introduction of the 1968 Race Relations Act. As this Act included discrimination in employment for the first time, (the 1965 Act made it unlawful to discriminate on grounds of race 'in places of public resort' only), a description of the situation before 1968 allows us to examine racial discrimination at work from a distance of 10 years of extended legislation.

The revelations of this Report in 1967 were as conclusive as they were unacceptable. An extensive programme of surveys and personal interviews with members of the black labour force showed that:

> Nearly half the West Indians claimed that they had personal experience of discrimination. Just over a third of both the Asian groups made similar claims. Only 6 per cent of Cypriots felt that they had ever been refused work unjustly.[7]

These findings were checked in a number of ways. A similar programme of investigations was carried out with employers, trade union representatives and the staff of private and public employment agencies. The researchers also set up experiments to look at discrimination in recruitment. Three applicants, one white English, one white Hungarian and one black, were rehearsed and sent to apply for a job offered by an organization claimed to be discriminating in the people it employed. In nine out of every ten cases chosen, the claims of immigrants that they had been refused work because of race or colour were found to be justified.[8]

This report in 1967 went on to list other findings which showed how racial minorities were discriminated against in the way they were employed. The country showed its distaste for this form of injustice and made an attempt to proscribe it through the passing of the 1968 Race Relations Act. Another extensive investigation[9] carried out in 1973 revealed the relative effectiveness of that piece of legislation and of the progress made, if any, during the intervening seven years.

The response of employing organizations

This second major enquiry was aimed primarily at discovering how far employers and trade unions had taken steps to prevent discrimination within the terms of the second Race Relations Act. On the basis of a survey of 283 employers, case studies involving 14 organizations and interviews with head office staff of 28 large employers and eight trade unions, it was possible for the researchers to state:

> Our findings show that few employers have taken steps to ensure that the 1968 Race Relations Act is complied with in their plants. However, the results of direct questions about the Act show that managers do not, in general, view it with hostility, and many of them think that it has given the racial minorities a better deal in employment.
>
> Asked whether the Act had had a good or bad effect on race relations in employment, the majority (64 per cent) of managers thought it made little difference, while about equal numbers thought it had had a good and bad effect (good: 19 per cent—bad: 16 per cent). However, a substantial proportion of informants (40 per cent) thought that the minorities had a better deal in employment as a result of the Act, while only 3 per cent thought they were actually worse off; the remainder thought the Act had made no difference.
>
> Only 5 per cent of plants said that they had changed their policies or practices in any way because of the Act, but 19 per cent of large plants having at least 500 employees said they had made changes.[10]

It appears, then, that the second Race Relations Act had

relatively little impact inside the country's employing organizations. This point was further illustrated by the study in the description it gave of patterns of employment for racial minorities. This seemed to have changed little over the years. For example:

Types of job done by racial minorities

It was found that a high concentration of racial minorities existed in non-skilled manual jobs (10 per cent of the overall work force in this category of employment) whereas a much lower concentration was found in non-manual jobs (3.2 per cent). In the case of male workers, this kind of distribution was even more pronounced: 67 per cent of the male minority work force were doing non-skilled jobs compared with only 37 per cent of the total workforce; and 14 per cent were doing non-manual jobs compared with 21 per cent of the total work force.

Labour shortage

Organizations which had labour shortages were found to be more likely to employ minority groups in high concentrations than those which did not have this problem. However, the fact that some plants did not employ minority workers could not in general be explained by an abundance of available labour.

Shift work

A strong tendency for black workers to work permanently on night shifts was revealed.

Racial mix

Indians tended to work in small plants where few other minority workers were employed, while Pakistanis tended to work in large plants where large numbers of minority workers (normally other Pakistanis) were also working. West Indians were found to be evenly distributed across locations of different sizes and across plants with large and small numbers of minority workers.

Supervision

Just over one fifth (22 per cent) of plants with manual workers claimed that they had at least one black superviser with white manual workers under him. The proportion of plants with at least one such supervisor was nearly twice as high (39 per cent) in situations where at least 5 per cent of the work force was black. A substantial proportion of plants having high concentrations of racial minorities had no black supervisors. For plants with at least 2 per cent minority group workers (that is, those which might be expected to have one black supervisor in some situation) 30 per cent were found to have at least one such supervisor, another 19 per cent had none but expected to have them within two years, while the remaining 51 per cent neither had any black supervisors nor expected to have any within the following two years.

Disadvantage

The existence of this pattern of employment for minority groups cannot be said to be proof of racial discrimination. For instance, the tendency for black workers to be found in concentrations on night shifts may be due to these workers preferring 'unsocial working hours' because of the higher earnings involved. The disproportionately low numbers of black supervisors might also be due to a variety of reasons other than (or additional to) racial discrimination. (This point is discussed in more detail in Part III.) Similarly, it is a fact that when unemployment rises, black workers are disproportionately affected; for example, between November 1973 and May 1975, the total number of unemployed rose by 65 per cent but the number of unemployed black workers rose by 156 per cent.[11] Once again, this may be attributable to more than crude prejudice on the part of employers. While the way black workers are distributed in employment may not be described as proof of discrimination, it does show undeniably that racial minorities are at a disadvantage in employment. In organizations where this disadvantage applies, managers whose job it is to understand and control parameters which affect the organization and its work force should want to know why this is the case.

No problems here

Although two particular studies have been used to display the statistics and features of racial discrimination and disadvantage in employment, a whole host of corroborating evidence is available from other sources.[12]

This information was a useful starting point for the study on which this book is based. Our investigation, however, was in no way aimed at discovering the extent of disadvantage or at proving discrimination. It was not meant to be a highly systematic piece of research on discrimination like the studies referred to previously, but was an attempt to find out about the managerial difficulties that were currently reputed to arise as a result of employing ethnic minority groups. We especially wanted to discuss these problems with managers (principally managers but also trade union representatives, black employees, white employees and people well versed in race relations in employment) and also to look into the options that existed for coping with them. The outcomes of this investigation are described in Part III but it seems appropriate to record here our findings about managerial attitudes towards race relations as these are pertinent to our review of the 'case for action'.

In the 22 organizations visited, a commonly encountered initial pronouncement was 'We have no racial problems here'. Further investigation often revealed that this opening statement could be given a different or extended interpretation. Sometimes it turned out to mean 'We do have problems but we don't like talking about them' or 'We do have problems but we are ignoring them' or 'We have no problems because there is no protest' or 'We don't have problems but our black employees do!'

It would be misleading to give the impression that all the managers consulted adopted such stances. In a substantial proportion of the organizations visited, management was well aware that racial problems and discriminatory practices were occurring on the firm's premises. Some of these managers had concluded that it was impossible or inadvisable for them to take action but others were determined to curtail discriminatory practices in the company. However, the overwhelming impression gained during the visits to organizations was of a disturbing lack of awareness in the face of obvious discrimination or severe disadvantage.

Lack of awareness

The attitudes of managers to race or colour are likely to vary along the same continuum of tolerance which seems to apply throughout our society. At one extreme, there are a few people who are fanatically prejudiced whilst at the other end of the spectrum there are those who are completely free of this sort of bias. The people at either extreme are much more likely to be aware (and to make others aware) of their attitudes to race than the great majority of the population who fall somewhere between these two polarized positions. Most people appear to give little thought to matters of race until the subject impinges on their lives in a personal way. In our study it appeared that managers did indeed show a variety of attitudes to race but it was noticeable how many of them were unaware of the impact of race on their own thinking and on the practices of their organizations. For example, when asked if the organization (a large national employer) had any black executives in a particular function, one senior manager replied, 'No, but we have a blind bloke if that will do.' A director insisted his company had no racial problems yet Wogs Out was daubed over walls on the shop floor. Often managers would say something like, 'The Asian workers are our best people. They keep themselves to themselves. They don't cause half as many problems as the whites. They have much better records for turnover, absenteeism and they'll always do anything that is asked of them. They don't seem to go through grievance and disciplinary procedures or complain so much as the whites either.' One manager said, 'We don't discriminate here. We will employ anybody so long as the work gets done.' A more typical example of the lack of awareness displayed by managers was the regularly heard assertion that 'You can see we don't discriminate. Just count the black faces on the shop floor.'

'White backlash' and 'benign neglect'

Those managers who were aware that discrimination occurred in their companies and yet did nothing to stop it gave several reasons for this passivity. The main reasons cited could be described as the 'white backlash' and the 'benign neglect' arguments.

Several managers expressed a fear that any move on their part to combat racial discrimination and disadvantage would certainly bring a hostile reaction from the white workers. It was said that such moves would be seen as a favouring of black employees. Some managers suggested that they did little to stop discrimination because of a wish not to expose their black workers to open hostility which, they believed, would inevitably result. It was also claimed that customers and clients would react adversely if black employees were to be used to represent the organization. Managers appeared to have little evidence for these beliefs and sometimes it seemed that the danger of generating resentment in employees or customers was only a projection of a manager's own reservations. In fact previous experience[13] seems to suggest that, while white workers may initially resent any positive attempts aimed at helping black workers overcome disadvantage, this is usually fairly easily dispelled provided that a just case for action exists.

The 'benign neglect' argument is slightly different. Managers do not say that they should and would like to do something yet are restrained by the attitudes of the workforce. Rather, they contend that it is wrong (or at best counter-productive) for managers to initiate action of this kind. The benign neglect precept holds that the interests of all concerned would be better served if the problems were left alone to resolve themselves 'naturally'. The benign neglect approach is now illegal but in any case, while it is possible that such an approach could be successful in certain circumstances, it is notable that there are few other areas apart from race where managers have ever advocated a policy of benign neglect. Further, it is interesting to speculate that if this line of thought were to be developed, a case could be made for declaring all managers redundant forthwith.

The call for action

So far, in examining the 'case for action', we have suggested that although there is widespread misinterpretation of information, the truth is racial discrimination and disadvantage are widely in evidence throughout employment. We have also said that extensive research, (and our own study), suggests that employers seem to have done little to change this situation and that managers tend to have small interest or awareness concerning race relations in industry. This is all the more surprising when the penalties associated with neglect and the potential benefits of taking action are considered.

Organizational effectiveness

Since the Industrial Revolution, the practice of management in employing organizations has changed fundamentally in response to social and political development. Another influence, behavioural science, has also helped mould modern management through revelations concerning the human side of enterprise. We know that to manage effectively in today's environment we must ensure that employees can satisfy some of their own needs and find outlets for talent and initiative whilst in pursuit of organizational objectives. This means that profitability, quality of service and so on will be dependent on organizational climate, on workforce morale and on the extent to which the abilities of all employees are nurtured and used. Bearing this in mind, it is easy to find numerous examples of organizations losing or limiting effectiveness by their tolerance of racial discrimination or disadvantage.

Neglecting human energy, talent or skill in any context is deplorable. Wasting such valuable resources in working situations is plain bad business. The company that refuses to take black workers on the ground of prejudice alone is quite clearly limiting the richness of its available labour market. Similarly, the organization that recruits black workers only when it is unable to get white labour to do a particular job or jobs is raising artificial barriers against the free flow of human potential. In places where black workers are confined to certain low levels or less pleasant functions in the organization, this undoubtedly represents wastefulness. The policy of keeping black workers to certain types of employment has been defended on the ground that no-one else will do the work. Even if this were true, it does not follow at all that when people show ability to do other work it is anything but in the best interests of the company for that potential to be recognized and fostered.

In our visits to companies, we saw many instances of money being wasted because of discrimination. Line managers refusing to take any of the black candidates sent to them by the personnel department because of prejudice means an extension of the expensive recruitment process. Searching around to find someone to promote when an eminently suitable black candidate is readily to hand is not only time-consuming and expensive in itself but also probably means that more difficulties than necessary will arise due to the promoted man's lower ability or less extensive knowledge of the work. If this promoted man has had to be taken from another function or department where he was performing well, the loss in the organization is further exacerbated. Similarly, ignoring obviously able black workers in making selections for training for more skilled work means that eventually a lower standard of skilled worker will be at the disposal of the organization. In industrial concerns that means lower production.

The penalties that result from ineffective communication at any level or in any function can be particularly severe in terms of organizational performance. On race relations, the barriers to communication might be obvious language problems, less clear cultural differences, or crude prejudice. If left unassailed such barriers can mean mistakes in that, quantitatively and qualitatively speaking, what is done turns out to be different from what was requested.

An aspect of discrimination that is almost universally lost on managers is the possibility that it adversely affects more than those who are its immediate victims. Many of the Germans who threw stones at Jewish people in the late 1930s would have done so not so much out of hatred for Jews but because of fears that, if they did not take part, the missiles might be hurled towards them instead. Also, the soldier who saw his neighbour shot as they left the trenches might think initially 'Thank heavens that wasn't me!' but the incident is unlikely to improve his relationship with the enemy! British industry suffers from its own version of trench warfare and the perceptions of 'them and us' between manager and worker are still highly damaging. This perceived manager-versus-worker conflict is undoubtedly one of the reasons why the productivity of the British worker using the same machinery is much lower than most of his Continental counterparts. It is our belief that when white workers witness management practising, condoning or tolerating the injustice of racial discrimination, their levels of trust and respect regarding management must be seriously impaired. Additionally, if workers observe management 'bending the rules' it would not be surprising to find them playing the same game. In this way the whole culture of the organization can be damaged. None of this can do anything to improve industrial relations or to bring about the boost in productivity that is so avidly demanded at this time.

Social responsibility

In a recent article on Social Responsibility; the Investment that Pays Off[14] Peach and Hargreaves, two senior executives with IBM, spoke of three distinct but interrelated levels of corporate responsibility. *Basic responsibilities* included paying taxes, satisfying the law and meeting the needs of stake-holders; the term *organizational responsibilities* was used to cover the company's need to minimize the negative aspects of its activities on the surrounding environment. The third level of corporate responsibility was termed *societal responsibilities.*

> It is at this level that business management is today facing new and urgent pressures, even though these pressures tend to be beyond the traditional expertise of management. They are, of course, the pressures of urban and environmental problems, of pressure groups and minorities, of inadequate institutions and so on. These are the factors that are having an increasing and dominant effect on the climate in which we can do business at all and which, if not controlled, make the efforts of even the best company management of marginal effect, and thus militate against its long-term profitability. To say that business must be

> involved in public and social affairs does not mean that it ceases to carry out the legitimate tasks it has always done. It simply means that, in the light of the new variables affecting its activities, it must review its investment mix so that a portion of its resources can be invested in building and maintaining the national fabric on which it and all other sections of society must depend. Investment in this way can be equated with money spent in research and management development: money spent today to protect the future.[15]

It is clear that a growing number of companies appreciate the validity of this argument. Although the cynic might suggest that the recently-born phenomenon of 'corporate advertising' is entirely political in origin, the 'Ideas In Action' of ICI and the Philips' 'Simply Years Ahead' approaches reveal the extent to which employing organizations are inextricably entwined in the development of society. They can contribute greatly to social progress but equally they may be the hardest hit institutional victims of social decay. As Peach and Hargreaves suggested, social responsibility is more than an indulgence in good works. It is:

> . . . the responsibility to plan and manage an organization's relationships with all those involved in or affected by its activities, or who can affect the ability of that organization to operate effectively.[16]

Although the social responsibility argument is most readily associated with giant industrial concerns, medium and small sized companies need also to accept a duty to their environment if they wish to operate successfully in the long-term. For example, a company's reputation in the local labour market greatly affects the quality of employee it can recruit. Its operations can also be influenced by local government and other authorities, the local press and radio.

The recognition by employers of their need to accept social responsibilities means that they must take action to eradicate racial discrimination. This will be done, not to impress overseas customers or suppliers but because taking on such responsibilities is necessary for immediate operational improvement and fundamental to the organization's long-term economic performance.

'Fire' prevention

On 26 January 1973 the Secretary of State for Employment asked the Commission on Industrial Relations (a body set up under the 1971 Industrial Relations Act) to examine and report on industrial relations in Mansfield Hosiery Mills Ltd. This request came after sustained and extensive coverage by the media of an industrial dispute by a group of the company's Asian workers who had already had a complaint to the Race Relations Board upheld. The dispute at the company's works in Loughborough in the winter of 1972 was largely a question of inequality of opportunity for certain Asian employees. As the Commission eventually reported:

> The dispute began with a wage claim by some Asian employees in June 1972 at the Trinity Street factory. It soon became apparent, however, that the real problem at issue was the lack of promotion opportunities to full-fashioned knitting jobs for Asian employees. After a one-week strike at the factory by the Asian bar-loaders, (unskilled work done in conjunction with skilled knitting jobs and performed exclusively by Asians at the time) in October 1972, the company agreed to promote two Asians but this was resisted by the white knitters. The problem

remained unresolved and the bar-loaders again withdrew their labour and on this occasion were joined by other Asians in both Loughborough factories. Agreement was reached in November, but when the Asians returned they found the company had recruited 41 white trainee knitters during the strike. The Asians again withdrew their labour, persuading the union concerned, the National Union of Hosiery and Knitwear Workers (NUHKW), to make the strike official although not all members joined in the strike. Further attempts to settle the problem failed and a Committee of Enquiry headed by Mr Kenneth Robinson was established on 7 December, 1972.[17]

The damage caused to the company by this extended episode was enormous. In addition to costly strikes, the company's operations were disrupted for several months. The harm to the firm's public image was immeasurable and the name Mansfield Hosiery is still always raised in any discussion on the possible penalties associated with practising or tolerating racial discrimination.

The Robinson Enquiry into the company was most thorough. Nine factories in the group were visited and detailed breakdowns of the organization prepared. The company's practices and policies were carefully scrutinized and manpower and earnings surveys were carried out. In its final report, the Commission endorsed the full Robinson enquiry list of recommendations for action by the company. On the principal reason for the dispute, it was urged that:

> . . . the company and the union should negotiate immediately a new training agreement which guarantees that the selection of trainee knitters shall be based on merit regardless of race, colour, creed or ethnic or national origin.[18]

This example of a 'fire' is perhaps the most infamous but is by no means the only case that could be cited. (Around the same time as the Mansfield Hosiery case two other major incidents occurred, at Imperial Typewriters in Leicester and at Birmid Qualcast in Birmingham.) These examples are perhaps extreme cases but they do serve as poignant reminders of what can happen if genuine grievances are not investigated and resolved by management. When underlying tension or conflict is neglected, it rarely dissipates of its own accord. It is much more likely to feed on itself until it finds release, often through some minor incident, with potentially very destructive consequences. Good management therefore involves the early identification and just treatment of all genuine grievances. This applies whatever the colour or ethnic origin of the employees in question.

There are two other aspects of the Mansfield Hosiery case which are worthy of note. First, when management tried to redeem themselves by promoting Asians to knitting jobs, white workers did resist this move. This in fact was hardly surprising since the dispute generated a great deal of 'racial' publicity. The clear division of the workforce into two groups, white skilled and Asian unskilled, would also have done much to produce this reaction.

The second point of interest is that at the time of the dispute the organization did not have at group or company level any manager exclusively responsible for personnel and industrial relations matters.

Management professionalism

Improving the effectiveness of managers has long been identified as a key factor in the creation of a stronger British economy. For this reason, and also for their own personal benefit, managers have themselves acknowledged the need to maintain and develop high standards of practice based on thoughtful application of theory and on utilization of skills gained through experience. Correspondingly, the concept of a 'professional approach' has been used in promoting managerial competence and in motivating managers to pursue their own development. In the case of personnel management, a professional institute was created and this now strives to increase the professionalism of the personnel function using various means which include the administration of a rigorous course of training and the setting of entrance examinations. Although some people dispute the appropriateness of this approach, there is no doubt that it is thought to be valid by a large number of managers as well as other interest groups in the employment and educational sectors.

A principal component of professionalism in almost every analysis is the commitment to an ethical code.[19] Doctors, lawyers and the other long-established professions have a strict code of conduct. These codes are fundamental to the individual's own sense of professionalism and to the invaluable public confidence he enjoys. If personnel specialists and other managers wish to possess more of such attributes, it seems that they too must take up some commonly agreed ethical position.

Since its inception in 1913, the Institute of Personnel Management has maintained that its members should concern themselves with both justice and effectiveness. The IPM has made numerous statements on issues relating to professional practice. For example, following the 1968 Act, the Institute made a detailed statement of policy on race relations in employment:

> Few people are confronted with the real implications of race relations in employment as frequently as personnel managers. The Institute believes that, as the

professional body representing personnel managers in this country, it has a special responsibility to work towards the long-term objectives of the Race Relations Act—racial harmony achieved by the total elimination of discriminatory practices. In its view, these objectives will best be achieved if personnel managers are personally committed to the Act and its intentions.[20]

Organizations have much to gain from managers adopting 'a professional approach'. For example, in personnel selection of any kind, the professional manager will use a systematic procedure to match candidate and job objectively. The technical know-how of the professional reduces the probability of any serious error in selection. It will ensure, for example, that although the selector feels favourably towards the candidate's family background, accent, social connections or ethnic origin, these characteristics will only influence selection when they are related to performance in the job. In this way the professional approach will serve well the needs of the organization.

For a number of reasons, the professionalism of personnel managers will be of particular importance in eliminating racial discrimination. In many organizations, the personnel function is already regarded as 'the most acceptable face of capitalism' and personnel managers will certainly feel a need to set an example on race relations that others might follow. Personnel managers will also represent the organization's interests in industrial tribunals or other settings where challenges and claims may be made on discriminatory practices. If this follows the same pattern as with, for example, claims of unfair or wrongful dismissal, the professionalism of the personnel manager will be of great importance to the organization. The personnel specialist could display his value to the organization even more forcefully by drawing attention to potential 'trouble spots' or areas of vulnerability *before* any complaint is made. The personnel function might also save management a further kind of embarrassment which we witnessed in our study. In one company, the union had taken up anti-discriminatory action unilaterally as it believed that the management of the firm would have no interest in joining such a campaign.

Legislation

The law provides another incentive for managers to take action against racial discrimination in the shape of the 1976 Race Relations Act. The ways in which the Act affects employment practices are discussed in Part II but it is important here, in looking at the case for action, to note what legislation aims to do and what in fact it can do:

> An Act of Parliament is an unequivocal declaration of public policy; as such it helps to establish general norms to which the law-abiding citizen will conform; it is accepted as a definition of good civic behaviour by a wide range of social institutions—trade unions, employers' associations, schools, voluntary associations and, above all, the family and the mass media. In short, an important part of the case for legislation is that not only will it put an end to overt discriminatory behaviour, but it will also help drive out prejudice. It is this latter goal with which a democratic society must be ultimately concerned and to reach it calls for more than legislation.[21]

Thus the occurrence of any major reduction in the levels of racial discrimination and disadvantage will depend on organizations pursuing *both* the letter and the spirit of the law. Relatively little will change if large numbers of managers continue to believe that the law is about unnecessarily costing the company money, about unfairly favouring a section of the community or about giving certain people even more of a chance to show 'a chip on the shoulder' at the expense of the enterprise. Regrettably, there is a possibility that this kind of response may occur to a greater extent than might be expected due to the 1976 Race Relations Act following a period of extensive legislation on employment. Laws on equal pay, employment protection, health and safety, sex discrimination, appeared quite closely together. This was greatly resented by some managers, who believed it restricted their capacity to manage effectively just at the time when the country was most in need. A much more positive interpretation was given by one manager in a discussion on race relations in employment:

> We know that legislation results from a long established democratic process and we all have an opportunity to express our views before any Bill proposed actually becomes law. In any particular period, the prevailing political persuasion might mean we end up disliking or liking a whole series of new laws but there is no question that the great majority of managers attempt to keep within the law. The difference is the amount of personal commitment we have and the subsequent attitudes we take. For example, a lot of managers believe that the Employment Protection Act has made it harder to manage well by restricting the number of options we have available to us. It seems to me that the actual outcome could be to make us better managers. If we cannot sack people so easily then it might mean we are more careful in selecting them in the first place. Similarly, it should also encourage us to structure the work better, be more concerned with properly motivating employees and do more to plan

ahead for our labour needs. At the end of the day we could all be better off.

We believe that the widespread adoption of this kind of positive approach will mean that multi-racial workforces are managed more effectively for the benefit of organizations, community and country.

PART II

THE RACE RELATIONS ACT 1976

Race relations legislation

The first attempt to outlaw racial discrimination was taken in 1965 when it became unlawful to discriminate unfairly in places of 'public resort'. After three years it was evident that further legislation was needed and the Race Relations Act 1968 extended the coverage of anti-discrimination legislation to include employment, housing and the provision of services. In this Act racial discrimination was defined as treating any person less favourably than another, on the grounds of colour, race or ethnic or national origins.

Employers were liable under the 1968 Act for any unlawful discriminatory acts of their employees, although in the event of court proceedings it would be a defence if they could show that they had taken 'such steps as were reasonably practicable to ensure compliance with the Act.' The principal feature of the arrangements made for enforcement of the law was an emphasis on conciliation. This can be seen from the procedure laid down for investigation of any complaint of racial discrimination relating to employers, trade unions or employers' organizations. A complaint had to be lodged with the Race Relations Board, the Department of Employment or one of the regional conciliation committees within two months of the alleged discriminatory act. All employment complaints were to be forwarded to the Department of Employment which would then set in motion one of two investigatory procedures. In the case of the 30 or so industries which had set up their own machinery to deal with complaints under the 1968 Act the Department of Employment passed on the complaint for investigation by the industry's own appropriate agency. Where no industry machinery existed the Race Relations Board was asked to take up the case and it was generally referred to one of the Board's regional conciliation committees.

A conciliation officer attached to the committee would obtain the complainant's case in full and he would then obtain the respondent's reply. If it was thought, on the balance of evidence, that unlawful discrimination had occurred a letter would be sent to the respondent setting out all the points which might be regarded as supporting the allegation made against him and asking him to comment on these in person or in writing or both: this was known as a pre-opinion letter. If it was thought that unlawful discrimination had not occurred then the pre-opinion letter would be sent to the complainant. When, in answer to the pre-opinion letter, the respondent or complainant had made his representations, the committee would consider the case. If it found the representations persuasive a pre-opinion letter would be sent to the other party. If not, it would form an opinion that unlawful discrimination had or had not occurred. If an opinion of unlawful discrimination was formed the committee would be under a statutory obligation to try to achieve a settlement between the parties and to obtain an assurance from the employer that he would not discriminate in a similar way in future.

The settlements arrived at have been varied in nature and have included damages, apologies, and re-instatement. Failure to get a satisfactory settlement and/or assurance meant that the case would go back to the Race Relations Board which would make a decision on whether or not to institute court proceedings.

The 1968 Act, in terms of its scope and its method of enforcement, was soon believed to be inadequate. The ethnic minorities themselves appeared to have little belief in the legislation and a common criticism was the long-windedness of the process of redress. Many people believed that a complaints-based process would always be inadequate as victims of discrimination often fail to make official complaints because of a fear of being embarrassed, becoming involved in official proceedings or being victimized. In addition there was a considerable volume of evidence which indicated that the 1968 Act was proving ineffective and that racial discrimination was still very much a feature of society. This was believed to be especially true about employment and both the Race Relations Board and the Community Relations Commission considered that the law was having less impact than was necessary in employing organizations. The Board gave one reason for this when it reported that:

> employment is an area in which discrimination is very difficult to establish. Compared with, say, service in a public house, it is often hard to determine what constitutes equality of treatment. The factors which influence management decisions are many and complex; and in the absence of more crude and overt forms of discrimination, it is usually extremely difficult to relate decisions directly to colour or origins.[22]

In contemplating further legislation the Government also took into account that in a troubled industrial climate it was necessary to try and prevent racial unrest causing further deterioration. A new Race Relations Act was also believed necessary in order to harmonize the legal machinery for dealing with unfair discrimination on the ground of race with that set up to prevent sexual discrimination. The Sex Discrimination Act, passed in 1975, had several features which were believed to represent a more effective means of combating discrimination than the arrangements laid down in the existing legislation on race.

For all these reasons it was clear that a new Race Relations Act was needed. This was widely recognized and eventually on 22 November 1976 the Royal Assent was given to a new Act which completely replaced the 1968 Act. This new Act did not come into force until mid-1977 when the Commission for Racial Equality became operational.

The Race Relations Act 1976

Definitions of discrimination in the 1976 Act

The Race Relations Act 1976 defines racial discrimination as follows:

> A person discriminates against another in any circumstances relevant for the purposes of any provision of this Act if:
>
> a) on racial grounds he treats that other less favourably than he treats or would treat other persons; or
>
> b) he applies to the other a requirement or condition which he applies or would apply equally to persons not of the same racial group as that other, but—
>
> i) which is such that the proportion of persons of the same racial group as that other who can comply with it is considerably smaller than the proportion of persons not of that racial group who can comply with it, and
>
> ii) which he cannot show to be justifiable irrespective of the colour, race, nationality or ethnic or national origin of the person to whom it is applied; and
>
> iii) which is to the detriment of that other because he cannot comply with it.[23]

This definition embraces several significant changes. For example, the 'racial grounds' concept used to define the unlawful nature of any 'less favourable treatment' was extended to cover nationality:

> This reverses the House of Lords decision in *Ealing London Borough Council v Race Relations Board*, and removes an important loophole in earlier legislation. Under the 1968 Act it was not unlawful to discriminate against someone because he was, for example, an Indian national, but it was unlawful to discriminate against him because of his Indian national origins. Consequently, the distinction between nationality and national origins created a pretext for discriminating on racial grounds. With certain appropriate exceptions it is unlawful under the 1976 Act to discriminate on grounds of nationality (and citizenship). This applies to EEC workers and their families under the Treaty of Rome, and to all aliens and Commonwealth citizens in this country.[24]

Apart from eliminating this loophole, the 1976 Act reaffirmed the illegality of direct racial discrimination in employment. Thus it remains unlawful for jobs to be refused, for differential rates of pay to be given, for selective dismissal or redundancy to be applied or for any other conscious single biased action to be shown towards any employee or prospective employee because of his ethnic or national origins. The 1976 Act also deems segregation on racial grounds as less favourable treatment. This holds even for circumstances where separate treatment is claimed to be equal treatment. If black workers are only offered work of a certain kind or given employment on only one shift, this constitutes unlawful discrimination. But it must be shown that the employer actively operated this kind of discrimination (for instance, by refusing black applicants to join or transfer to other shifts or departments), and not that any segregation was simply a result of free choice exercised by members of ethnic minorities. (Segregation is permissible for purposes of affirmative action and this is discussed later.)

Several managers consulted during our investigation appeared to believe that direct racial discrimination was defensible when demanded by customers or other workers. According to the law, racial discrimination cannot be practised as a means of resolving other conflicts or in the interests of commercial performance; also, customers and employees can contravene the law by inciting others to discriminate unfairly.

Indirect discrimination

Perhaps the most significant change in the legal definition of racial discrimination brought by the 1976 Act was the prohibition of so-called 'indirect discrimination'. This concept, which was also used in the Sex Discrimination Act 1975, refers to the imposing of any condition or requirement which, although applied equally to persons of all racial groups, has a differential effect because the proportion of a particular racial group who can comply with it is considerably smaller than that for other groups. Where such a condition or requirement cannot be shown (by the person applying it) to be justifiable irrespective of the racial group of those to whom it is applied, it constitutes an unlawful indirect discriminatory practice.

In discussing this change in the law with managers we found that many of them were greatly surprised to learn that they and their organizations could be found guilty of discriminating when they have had no *intention* to discriminate against ethnic minorities. Discrimination in their minds was identified with prejudice. Their thinking was heavily orientated towards motive and they were relatively unaware of unintentional but unjustifiable discrimination *in effect*. On reviewing the implications of this, several managers said that they might have to reconsider their 'no problems here' remarks and a number of their common employment practices did seem highly suspect on indirect discrimination. The points most commonly emerging, which are discussed in detail in Part III, included the levels of literacy required in over-demanding application forms; stringent language proficiency requirements; some selection tests; and criteria and methods of advertising used in selection for promotion or skills training.

There is undoubtedly a good deal of scope for interpretation of when and where unlawful indirect discrimination may have occurred. (A major item is what can be deemed 'justifiable conditions or requirements'.) This should become clearer as precedents are built up in courts and tribunals.

It should be remembered that in cases of alleged indirect discrimination the burden of providing proof to courts and tribunals that a condition or requirement is justifiable is on the alleged discriminator. (The complainant has to prove everything except justifiability.) This makes it even more important for managers to acquaint themselves fully with their organizational practices and the way they operate *vis à vis* ethnic minorities. (If he can show that there was no intention to discriminate, an employer would not have to pay compensation to a victim who brought a successful complaint before a tribunal.)

Discrimination without a victim

Under the 1976 Act a Commission for Racial Equality (CRE) was formed. This Commission (and only the CRE) can ask an organization to account for 'potentially discriminatory practices'. In other words the existence of a victim is not necessary and an organization may be taken to court on the basis of any of its practices which *would* constitute indirect discrimination if there was a victim available to testify to this.

Victimization

The definition of discrimination also covers victimization of any person complaining of less favourable treatment under the Act. This clause on victimization, which is also present in the Sex Discrimination Act 1975, was inserted because of the well-known reluctance on the part of most victims to take action against racial discrimination because of the fear of reprisals.

Liability under the Act

Under the 1976 Act employers remain liable for the discriminatory acts of employees whether or not these were carried out with the employer's consent or knowledge. An employer can successfully defend himself if he can satisfactorily show that all 'reasonably practicable' steps were taken to prevent such acts occurring. (In several cases brought by the Race Relations Board this was interpreted as ensuring that all employees knew that racial discrimination would not be tolerated within the organization but this has not been properly tested in the courts.) The 1968 Act made it unlawful for trade unions to commit certain acts of discrimination against applicants for membership or against members. This section also covered 'any person concerned with the affairs' of a trade union, and in this way shop stewards were covered. The 1976 Act contains no mention of 'any person concerned with the affairs' of a union and so shop stewards escape. But if a shop steward instructs, incites or induces discrimination, he is as liable as anyone else. Moreover, as far as *liability* is concerned, trade unions and shop stewards will continue to be bound by the provisions relating to principals and agents although the difficulty here is that it rarely happens that it can be shown, in cases of alleged discrimination, that a shop steward has been acting as an agent of the trade union and with its authority. The Act also covers employers associations, professional or trade organizations, employment agencies, careers advisory services, partnerships (partnerships of six or more partners will be covered on the selection and treatment of partners), qualifying or licensing bodies and the Manpower Services Commission and its agencies. The Act is also binding on the Crown, and Crown employees are protected by the Act.

Scope in employment

The scope of the 1976 Act in employment is much greater than in previous legislation. As far as recruitment is concerned, it is unlawful to discriminate against a job applicant in any arrangements made for advertising, offering the job or selecting the candidate, in the terms offered, (this represents a difference from the Sex Discrimination Act as terms and conditions are covered by the Equal Pay Act), or by refusing or deliberately omitting to offer employment on racial grounds. It is also unlawful to instruct, pressure or aid another person to discriminate. Employees, the self employed and contract workers (with some refinements) are all protected from racial discrimination regarding the terms of employment; the opportunities for training or promotion or transfer; and dismissal.

Exceptions

So far as employment is concerned the Act applies to

organizations in Great Britain but not to those in Northern Ireland. Employees who work wholly or mainly outside Great Britain are exempt as are seamen who were recruited or engaged abroad. Seamen and aircrews recruited in Great Britain are covered by the Act. Employees not normally resident in this country who are employed in order to train in skills which are to be used outside Great Britain, or who intend to return to their country of origin on completion of the training, are not included.

All the provisions of the Act (except the clause on victimization) do not apply to employment in private households although workers contracted to provide services to private households are covered. The Act does not apply to social clubs or associations with less than 25 members and clubs who exist to provide benefits to members of a particular racial group also get some exemption so long as membership is not defined by reference to colour.

Discrimination is allowed in situations where being a member of a particular racial group can be regarded as a 'genuine occupational qualification'. Some examples cited are:

1 Acting—in entertainment where people of a particular racial group are necessary for purposes of authenticity
2 Artistic or photographic modelling—also for reasons of authenticity
3 Work in restaurants—where members of a certain racial group are needed to provide and reinforce any special atmosphere or setting, eg Greek, Chinese or Italian waiters in the appropriate restaurants
4 Welfare and social work—where personal welfare or social services for members of racial groups are most effectively provided by other members of that racial group.

None of these exceptions apply in situations where an employer can fill vacancies from existing employees who are members of the racial group in question.[25]

Discrimination, according to nationality, place of birth or residence, is also possible in some circumstances in games, sports and competitions. Charities may also give benefits selectively to racial groups so long as the group is not defined by reference to colour.

Affirmative action

Perhaps the most significant exception to the Act concerns the freedom given to employers, training agencies and unions to take affirmative action in order to promote or encourage the entry of particular racial groups into areas of work where they are considerably under-represented. These provisions are as follows:

1 A training body or agency is able to provide training solely for any particular racial group which is under-represented, either nationally or in any part of the country or in any particular occupation.

2 An employer or trade union can provide training for only those employees or members who are members of a particular racial group in order to fit them for work in which the group is under-represented (or where there is no one of that racial group doing the work)

3 An employer or union can encourage members of a particular group to take advantage of opportunities to do work in which that group is under-represented

4 A union can encourage members of a particular racial group only if it is under-represented among its members generally.

Under-representation in this context refers to the position in the previous 12 months and can be related to either number of employees (or union members) or to the proportion of the relevant population or labour market consisting of the racial group in question. These provisions could therefore be used to favour white employees, as well as minorities, in the appropriate circumstances.[26]

This exception for affirmative action allows an employer to assist members of a particular racial group only in order to eliminate inequality and disadvantage. It cannot be used to give advantage to particular racial groups and discrimination is not allowed at the point of recruitment. Similarly, other workers cannot be dismissed or similarly disadvantaged in order to increase opportunities for members of certain racial groups. The basic principle of the Act is equality of treatment for all.

Removal of the racial balance clause

A controversial feature of the 1968 Act was the 'racial balance' clause. This clause made it lawful for an employer to discriminate in order to prevent any job, department or shift becoming identified with a particular racial minority group. (The clause did not apply to persons wholly or mainly educated in Great Britain, no matter what their race.) The rationale of including such a clause was straightforward. It would not, it was argued, be in the interests of integration if members of racial minority groups, and particularly immigrants, were concentrated almost exclusively in particular parts of the organization. The 1968 Act therefore gave managers the right to take action to prevent this occurring so long as this was done in the interests of promoting racial harmony.

The 'racial balance' clause was not retained in the 1976 Act and employers may no longer lawfully operate a policy of limiting the proportion of workers from particular racial groups in any part of the organization nor any similar scheme aimed at securing a racial mix throughout the workforce. (The exception to this is affirmative action where the organization may take special steps to meet the needs of members of particular racial groups.) The exclusion of this clause did not meet with unanimous approval. The Government sided with the view that the clause was having little beneficial effect and that it might in fact be a source of considerable abuse and misunderstanding.

The Commission for Racial Equality (CRE)

A new Commission for Racial Equality was created by the 1976 Act. This Commission (which is similar in several ways to the Equal Opportunities Commission established under the Sex Discrimination Act 1975) superseded both the Race Relations Board and the Community Relations Commission. The CRE more than covers the functions and responsibilities of these two preceding agencies and has substantially greater powers than either of them. The Commission does not have the old Board's obligation to investigate every individual complaint, 'which should allow it more freedom to carry on its important strategic role in eliminating patterns of discrimination'.[27]

David Lane, former Conservative Member of Parliament for Cambridge, was appointed first Chairman of the CRE. The Commissioners, who are appointed by the Home Secretary on a full or part-time basis, will assist, guide and advise in much the same manner as in the Equal Opportunities Commission, the Health and Safety at Work Commission and other similar agencies. The staff of the CRE will not be civil servants although they will be paid by the Government. Provision was made for the CRE to be staffed initially from the existing employees of the Community Relations Commission and the Board so that their expertise and experience should not be lost.

Duties of the CRE

The main duties of the CRE are:

1 to work towards the elimination of discrimination
2 to promote equality of opportunity and to develop good race relations
3 to keep under review the working of the 1976 Act and to propose amendments whenever appropriate.[28]

The Commission will fulfil these duties by performing a number of different roles:

i) An enforcement role—it can issue non-discrimination notices, and bring proceedings in tribunals and courts
ii) An investigative role—it can conduct formal investigations and issue reports and recommendations, and in doing so it will have the power to require the furnishing of written information and to summon witnesses
iii) An educational role—it can run seminars and conferences etc
iv) An advisory role—it can advise individuals who have complaints. It can also advise employers and trade unions on equal opportunities
v) A research role—it can conduct research into companies or industries and also into matters outside the scope of the legislation
vi) A management role—it has the role of providing resources of money and expertise to Community Relations Officers
vii) A representative role—it can assist and represent individual complaints in appropriate cases.[29]

With the Home Secretary's and the Treasury's approval the CRE may provide resources to any agency which is attempting in any way to develop equal opportunity. (This includes research and educational activities.) The Commission is also committed to producing an Annual Report which will be presented to Parliament and published.

Codes of practice

The Commission is empowered to generate and issue codes of practice for employers. These codes will contain practical guidance on eliminating racial discrimination and promoting equality of opportunity. The codes will be prepared following consultation with all interested parties and will be viewed by Parliament. Any code of practice issued by the CRE will have similar status to that of the Industrial Relations Code of Practice under the Trade Union and Labour Relations Act 1974. This means that although it will not itself have the force of law the code will be admissible in evidence in tribunals. Tribunals may also refer to the code whenever it is relevant to the point at hand. Thus the CRE's code of practice will be of considerable assistance and guidance to employers. For instance, the guidance given in a code of practice about measures to be taken in order to prevent employees discriminating may, if sincerely pursued, help employers avoid liability for any such act carried out without their knowledge or consent. It will also assist in the application of equal opportunity policies.

Enforcement of the Act

Some of the powers of the Commission have already been briefly referred to in the description of its major roles. Perhaps the most significant of these powers is the CRE's ability to carry out formal investigations at its own discretion or at the request of the Home Secretary or Secretary of State for Scotland.

Formal investigations

These investigations may be conducted for any purpose connected with the Commission's duties. The scope of the investigation may be wide (for example, a study into national, regional or local issues) or they may be more specific (an organization or an individual).

The Commission is required to follow a set of procedures on these formal investigations but it need not wait for a complaint before initiating such a study. Any person (or specific organization) who is to be the subject of a formal investigation will be notified of the CRE's belief that he or she has committed an unlawful discriminatory act and of the intention to hold an investigation. (The Commission may investigate a person without believing that he or she has acted unlawfully.) The alleged discriminator may also be told of his right to make oral or written representations on his own behalf and of his right to be represented by counsel or a solicitor or a nominated person acceptable to the CRE, but the Commission is not legally obliged to do this. In those investigations set in motion by the Secretary for State or where a named person is thought to have committed an unlawful act the CRE can subpoena witnesses to attend the proceedings or provide relevant documentation. However, a witness may only be asked to provide such information as he would normally be required to give in civil proceedings.

In the case of proposed investigations where a person or organization is not named, the CRE is required to give general notice. The power to subpoena in these investigations is only available if the Home Secretary gives his authority. The Commission must prepare a report on each investigation it undertakes. For those studies initiated by the Home Secretary a report must be sent to the Government, whose duty it is to publish the findings. In other cases the CRE is required to publish the report or make it available for inspection. The CRE has a number of powers available which allows it to take action either during or after an investigation.

Non-discrimination notices

Where a formal investigation discloses an unlawful act of discrimination or potentially discriminatory practice, an unlawful advertisement or instructions or pressure to discriminate, the Commission may issue a 'non-discrimination notice' requiring that these acts cease. Before issuing the notice the recipient must be told of the Commission's intentions and its reason for so doing. The recipient must be given the opportunity to make oral or written representations which, if made within 28 days, must be taken into account by the CRE before it proceeds with the issue of a notice. These notices may be issued without the CRE having to go to court but they cannot result in any penalty except by court order.

If in order to comply with a notice a person or organization has to make changes in arrangements, the Commission has to be informed when these changes have taken place. The CRE can lay down the time and manner in which such notification of compliance is to be provided. If the recipient believes the notice to be unreasonable he has six weeks in which to appeal to an industrial tribunal. It is up to the appellant to prove his case in such appeals. The Commission may also conduct follow-up investigations up to five years after the notice to see if it is being complied with. It retains the power to subpoena in order for it to do this. A register of non-discrimination is kept and this record is available for public inspection.

Injunctions

If the recipient of a notice is believed to be likely to act unlawfully again, the CRE can apply to a county court (or sheriff court) for an injunction to restrain the recipient from persisting with his unlawful behaviour. This power, which does not depend on the Commission having conducted a formal investigation in the first place, only applies up to five years after the original non-discrimination notice was finally issued.

Individual complaints

The policy in the 1976 Act is to reserve all interpretation of the employment provisions to tribunals.[30] Hence, any person who alleges discrimination has occurred under the employment provisions of the 1976 Act must complain to the Central Office of Industrial Tribunals within three months of the alleged act. (In some circumstances late applications will be admitted.) Although the complainant may seek the advice and help of the CRE prior to his complaint this is the only route (except for a few minor exceptions) through which complaints of racial discrimination in employment may be channelled. Cases concerning discriminatory advertisements, and instructions or pressure to discriminate in employment, can only be put before a tribunal by the CRE.

Copies of all complaints made to the Secretary of Tribunals are immediately sent to the Advisory Conciliation and Arbitration Service (ACAS). A conciliation officer may then try to settle the case without the need for a tribunal (for example, by use of any existing grievance machinery). Any information or views given to the conciliation officer is confidential and may not be used in a tribunal without prior consent being given. No one is bound to consult or communicate with a conciliation officer and there is no prejudice associated with refusing such contact.

An individual may present his own case to a tribunal or he may choose a representative. This may be a solicitor, a member of a minority association, a trade union official or some other acceptable representative. A complainant may seek help from the CRE which has power to assist individuals in certain circumstances.

In most instances the onus of providing proof of less favourable treatment falls on the complainant but, in claims of indirect discrimination, it is the respondent who has to provide evidence of justifiability on non-racial grounds of any condition or requirement. It should be noted that:

> It is for the respondent in all cases to raise any statutory defences or exceptions. The tribunal will decide all issues (and the case) on the civil test of the balance of probabilities: not the criminal one of proof beyond all reasonable doubt.[31]

Another important point for employers to note is that

they have only 14 days after receiving a copy of the complaint form (IT 1) to give notification that they intend to fight the case. Failure to 'enter an appearance' by completing another form (IT 3) means that the employer will not be allowed to defend the case.

Question forms

In order to help a complainant find out how the respondent will reply to the complaint and so assist him to decide whether or not to bring proceedings, a 'question and answer' procedure has been devised. This involves the use of standard questionnaires which should help complainants decide how best to present their case. It is not compulsory to use these forms but on certain occasions the timing and nature of the question and answer procedure may be laid down. All the information gathered in this procedure may be used as evidence in a tribunal.

Remedies for discrimination

After the hearing the tribunal will declare the rights of the parties. In cases where unlawful discrimination is deemed to have taken place the tribunal may award compensation up to a maximum of £5,200. The calculation of this compensation will be different to that in unfair dismissal appeals to industrial tribunals as compensation for 'injury to feelings' may also be awarded. The tribunal may also recommend certain actions that the respondent must take within a specified period in order to rectify any injury done to the complainant. If these recommended actions are not complied with the amount of cash awarded in compensation may be increased.

PART III

MANAGEMENT AND THE MULTI-RACIAL WORKFORCE

Introduction

The Race Relations Act 1976, together with the need for increased organizational effectiveness, makes it imperative that managers regularly review their own practices on ethnic minorities. The major issues concerning management of the multi-racial workforce which emerged in our study are given here as they may provide some indication to managers of the sort of areas that should be explored initially. We use the word 'issues' because there is a high probability that failure to face them and to manage them justly and effectively will result in undesirable outcomes for the whole organization. As described earlier, the resultant penalties can be multifarious, ranging from poor organizational climate and reduced effectiveness to litigation and extensive adverse publicity.

For ease of presentation these issues concerning management of the multi-racial workforce have been categorized according to recruitment and selection; promotion and transfer; induction and training; and industrial relations. This account is followed by some points on 'equal opportunity policies', a few suggestions for 'affirmative action' and a discussion on monitoring and record keeping.

Recruitment and selection

The matter of recruitment and selection is perhaps the clearest example of how heavily an organization relies on its environment. All organizations must at some time recruit new employees; for the majority of jobs in most enterprises, recruits will come from the immediate 'travel to work area'. In some urban local labour markets, the proportion of black people in the working population is much higher than elsewhere. Often the concentration of ethnic minority residents in these areas has occurred rapidly and organizations can remain unaware of this trend until they suddenly discover that they employ much larger numbers of black workers than they ever imagined. Some employers, finding themselves in this position, have become very alarmed, especially when they see that the candidates presenting themselves for job interviews appear to be almost exclusively black.

Large proportions of ethnic minority workers in a workforce may also appear for a number of reasons in addition to changes in the composition of the local labour market. For example, because of the difficulty they have in getting employment, black workers will sometimes do unpleasant jobs or work unsocial hours more readily than other workers. Similarly, they will often take jobs which are too lowly-paid to attract other workers. Black workers may also come to form a substantial proportion of employees because of company policies or practices, such as voluntary redundancy programmes. (Various instances have been reported where ethnic minority workers have been less keen to accept voluntary redundancy due to the difficulty they expect to face in getting another job or because of financial commitments such as mortgages.)

Whatever the cause, it is possible that organizations can find themselves with quickly-growing proportions of ethnic minority employees. This phenomenon generated concern in the minds of a number of managers we consulted. These managers believed (and some cited anecdotal evidence) that their existing white employees were seriously perturbed by this trend. It was felt that many of their white workers would leave, so depriving the company of some of its best, most skilled long-service employees. It was further believed that, if the company became known as a 'black employer', it would become increasingly difficult for it to recruit and to retain white workers. We also heard the suggestion that allowing the company to become too heavily reliant on a certain ethnic minority group would mean the organization could be more easily 'held to ransom' because of the higher cohesiveness of that minority group compared to other workers. Consequently management decided that, in the commercial interests of the enterprise, it would need to intervene and curtail the growth in the number of black employees. Hence irrespective of merit the entry of black workers into the organization was restricted until a 'reasonable balance' was restored. The precise dimensions of this balance appear often not to be rationally determined (say, for example, by matching the balance in the local labour market). The number of black workers that managers believe an organization can accommodate appears frequently to be based on intuitive

school leaver cycle or other factors. This means that in terms of recruitment organizations simply react to the current conditions prevailing in the labour market. As a result, sometimes the company will find it easy to obtain the number and type of employee it requires and at other times this will be extremely difficult, if not impossible. Consequently recruitment policies tend to be dynamic.

At the time of our study it appeared that, due to the plentiful supply of non-skilled or semi-skilled labour, many organizations were increasing their standards for entry. While this can be said to be right and proper generally, it is not at all defensible when it means that black workers are unfairly discriminated against. It is well-known that the levels of unemployment for black workers (especially young blacks) are usually higher than for the rest of the population. Some people would claim that this is due in some part to the differences in cultural or sub-cultural factors, educational standards and so on. Irrespective of the merit or otherwise of this argument there is plenty of research evidence to prove that some employers do discriminate against ethnic minority applicants. We can assume that this is unquestionably a factor contributing to the black unemployment level. This sort of racial discrimination and also unintentional indirect discrimination can arise at several points in the recruitment and selection process.

Recruitment and selection process

As we have already seen, the majority of the ethnic minority working population is employed in non-skilled occupations. Organizations tend to recruit these categories of employees from a variety of channels but mainly through the Department of Employment (Employment Services Agency's Job Centres), by local advertising, using notice-boards outside the factory or through personal referral. Earlier race relations legislation ruled out racial discrimination in any method of recruitment but, as the number of complaints to the Race Relations Board[32] has consistently shown, deliberate discrimination often occurs when black applicants first contact an organization. Applicants have been known to be rejected out of hand by telephonists, receptionists and gate-keepers. (In our look at 22 organizations, two cases of gate-keepers turning away black applicants were described. Both men were disciplined by the companies concerned.) Complaints to the Race Relations Board have by no means been confined to accusations of prejudice on the part of this level of employee. Managers have regularly been accused of rejecting applicants peremptorily on discovering that they belonged to a racial minority. This kind of prejudice can be very harmful to the organization by its artificial limitation on incoming talent. It is also unlawful. Thus organizations should make sure that *all* enquiries or applicants are passed on to someone who is competent to deal with them objectively. The practice of keeping a record book of callers and applicants is an aid to removing some of the worst examples of this sort of abuse.

These instances of deliberate discrimination are, of course, not the only way on which a black applicant's chances of getting a job may be unjustly limited. The selection process is basically about getting a good matching of job and person. Thus the starting point of selection is a thorough analysis of the job in question. From this analysis, a 'job description' can be devised and then a 'personnel specification' may be compiled. By objectively following this procedure, a manager can identify the factors which are most relevant to good performance on the job. Diligence in following proper procedure will reduce the possibility of indirect discrimination and should also stand the organization in good stead if it has to face a complaint in an industrial tribunal.

The application form

The typical selection process starts when an applicant first contacts the manager responsible for selection. (For the sake of brevity, we will assume that this is the personnel officer.) Some initial and informal screening may take place but in most instances the next step is completion of an application form. When this has been scrutinized and the personnel officer is satisfied that the applicant is a likely candidate for the job, an interview will usually be arranged. At both these stages, application form and interview, direct and indirect discrimination may occur.

An application form may represent a difficult hurdle for an applicant of low educational standard. Some ethnic minorities (especially those schooled in less developed countries) understandably have a fear of the application form and it seems that some people go as far as to try to avoid this particular part of the selection process. On our visits to organizations we were given examples of application forms being spirited away from personnel offices so that they could be filled in by others on behalf of applicants, who then submitted the completed forms as their own work. An applicant would also, it seems, sometimes arrive with a friend who surreptitiously completed the form. We came across an instance where an Asian successfully negotiated the selection process but another Asian turned up to do the job.

These incidents were reputed to be common and we saw a variety of measures used by organizations to counter this type of behaviour. For example, a secretary or receptionist might be assigned to watch each applicant and ensure that the right person completed the form. One personnel department went so far as to have a 'peep-hole' scratched in the middle of a painted-over glass partition so that black applicants might be watched while completing the forms.

The personnel managers concerned said that they were unwilling to take such measures but they did so because of the importance that had to be placed on the application form. For this level of employee, selection is heavily dependent on the application form since a well-designed form is the most efficient yet cost-effective method by which a manager can make quick assessments. It is the quickest and cheapest way of asking whether an applicant has the essential attributes (for example, work experience, good working record, training, knowledge of the industry etc) to do the job. With black applicants, it appears that in some cases more attention is paid to the way in which the form is completed than to the information it is designed to elicit. In other words, the applicant's skill in completing the form is given heavier emphasis than his qualifications for doing the job. Whilst there are many jobs where the abilities to read and write well are fundamental to job performance, it is difficult to see how, for example, the fact that an applicant cannot spell the name of his last employer is in any way an indicator of his or her ability to operate a knitting machine or press.

Nearly all the managers we spoke to were adamant that all future employees would be required to have a basic level of competence in reading and writing English. This would be a condition covering all applications for jobs irrespective of racial or educational background. Several reasons were given for making this stipulation: in the interests of safety, employees needed to be able to read safety-warning notices; it is impossible to pass on all information by word of mouth and written notices are the usual means by which an organization communicates officially with employees (for example, written warnings in disciplinary procedures); in an age of fast-changing technology, even the lowest-grade employee would at some time have to go through training or take up a job which involved reading or writing; similarly, promotion to supervisor or above would be impossible for someone who was analphabetic.

Few people would deny that these arguments have validity. Nevertheless, to operate a blanket requirement on reading and writing for all jobs may in fact be inappropriate and in some instances might constitute unfair discrimination. In one organization we visited, it had long been the company's policy to ask for good levels of literacy in English. For a number of years, the company had in fact taken on many recently-arrived Asian immigrants who were said to be excellent workers. In screening Asian applicants for jobs, considerable emphasis was placed on literate completion of the application form and the recruitment officer also checked reading ability by asking each applicant to look at a particular paragraph of the works rule book. The applicant would then be asked to say in his or her own words what the paragraph was about. After using the same paragraph for many months, the recruitment officer decided to change the example to a less well-worn page in the rule book. He was staggered to find that on asking an Asian applicant to say what the new paragraph was about, the applicant reeled off the contents of the old paragraph.

This incident would suggest that in all probability the company's required standards for competence in reading and writing had not been met by all its existing employees, yet the performance of the Asian workforce had been more than satisfactory. Thus the relevance of the company's demands on literacy was called into question. Justifying such selection requirements is not as straightforward as some managers would seem to assume.

The interview

Some of these points concerning reading and writing skills for the application form also apply to verbal fluency and dialect for the interview.

Nearly all the organizations we visited had a policy of not accepting any job applicant who appeared incapable of expressing himself ably in English. This requirement had not always been applied (we saw several instances of Asian employees who spoke little English and some managers were frank enough to say that they could only apply this language proficiency condition because of the current levels of unemployment). Those managers who were demanding higher language standards justified this on the grounds that it would help reduce errors caused by poor communication and would improve work relations generally.

Few people would disagree that it is infinitely preferable for all people in the organization to speak a common language but the fact that many organizations had already successfully employed workers who did not speak good English suggests that the necessity of applying such a reqirement cannot be taken for granted. Organizations need to look closely at just how fluent a worker needs to be to do particular jobs. (The question of language training is discussed later under 'training and development.')

The frailties of the interview as a selection tool are well-known and almost every experienced manager will be aware of 'halo' effects and the converse phenomena. Eliminating this sort of bias is difficult in practice. An interviewer will often be attracted or offended by aspects of a candidate's speech, physical appearance, dress or manner. While he has every right to have such feelings, he has a professional responsibility to see that these only influence the selection decision when they are relevant to performance in the job. From our study, it seems probable that in the interview and throughout the selection process ethnic minorities could be treated more fairly if selection criteria were job-related and were, whenever possible, derived objectively and systematically.

In discussing with managers what might be done to prevent ethnic minorities suffering excessively from conscious or unconscious bias, the subjectivity of the way in which most selection decisions were arrived at was highlighted. Some managers defended this on the ground that it was just as important to get someone who suited the organization and its culture as to recruit someone who could do the job. It will be interesting to see how this matter is dealt with by industrial tribunals since it seems quite clear that variations from job-related criteria can constitute unlawful indirect discrimination. We believe that organizations will need to produce much more reasoned and substantiated arguments than they appear to do at present if they are to justify some aspects of their recruitment and selection policies.

Qualifications and experience

We found several examples of personnel departments giving 'spot checks' only to black applicants who claimed to have had relevant experience or qualifications. This was done because many managers seemed to have had some encounter with a black applicant who exaggerated or falsified such data. Some personnel managers had developed their own indicators of whether the applicant's claims were genuine. The checks which were aimed at a particular skill (reading a micrometer for someone claiming to be a craftsman) seemed to have more validity than those which were meant to find out about more academic qualifications (general knowledge questions).

This kind of checking tended only to be used for Asian applicants as there seemed to be a widespread assumption that Asians were in the habit of 'trying it on'. One personnel manager said, 'I've got five BA Calcuttas sweeping up in this works.' This was typical of the attitude of several others. Very often, personnel managers started an interview with an Asian with the assumption that his or her experience or qualifications (especially when gained overseas) were dubious. As in some cases it is too difficult, costly or time-consuming to verify an applicant's claimed experience or qualifications (for example, finding out whether the applicant spent five years in a bank in Bombay or assessing exactly what a particular degree from a Pakistani university entails) this basic assumption can mean an applicant is unfairly disadvantaged. If this means he is rejected, the company loses a potentially good employee. It also takes a chance of a complaint of racial discrimination being brought against it. The applicant who claims overseas qualifications is unlikely to be taken on even for a job very much below his capabilities, as managers are aware of the risk that he or she will eventually agitate for a better job and so in all probability prove an unsettling influence. Nowadays, selection mistakes are difficult and costly to 'rectify' and organizations are unwilling to take risks. This heightened caution might mean that immigrants are even further disadvantaged and even though a manager may have experienced a greater tendency to overstate qualifications or experience amongst a certain racial group, it is wrong to attribute such behaviour to all members of that group.

It would be unrealistic to expect organizations to apply anything more than 'rules of thumb' on this question of overseas experience and qualifications and some means of assisting organizations in this ought to be considered by the relevant national agencies. But there is no doubt that assuming all or most 'exotic' experience or qualifications to be false or meaningless is unfair. This is therefore another area where organizations will need to review their present practices and to find out whether they can be justified.

Selection testing

There was little evidence of formal selection tests (performance measures of intelligence, aptitude, personality) being used for ethnic minorities in the companies included in our investigation. This was principally because most of these people were taken on for non-skilled or semi-skilled work. We did encounter a few examples which were mainly concerned with clerical workers. It was not possible for a detailed analysis to be made on these tests but the managers seemed to think there could be instances (usually said to be minor in nature) where these tests discriminated in a way they were not supposed to. Certain tests have been shown to discriminate unfairly against women and it is likely that some tests will also contain cultural bias.* In the United States, attempts have been made to eliminate this sort of discrimination and tests are now standardized locally so as to give each ethnic minority a chance to be fairly

*A description of how selection tests themselves, or misuse of selection tests can operate against ethnic minority groups is given in Dr Michael Pearn's ITRU research paper (SL8) *Selection Tests for Immigrant Workers—Some Problems of Administration and Interpretation*, and in his TSA paper *Selecting and Training Coloured Workers* (HMSO 1977)

compared with others. Organizations in this country who rely extensively on selection tests can carry out their own check of whether the tests they use contain any obvious discriminatory elements but proof of impartiality will probably have to come from more extensive research. In the meantime, a decision will have to be made on whether the advantages brought by any particular test outweigh the potential penalties it can incur through being discriminatory on racial grounds.

Line management

The candidate's interview with the personnel manager will usually be followed by a short meeting with a line manager or supervisor, who will have the final say on selection. Our investigations showed that this is the point in the selection process when prejudice is most often revealed. It may be that this is an artificial impression created because we talked mainly to personnel managers but we did come across several examples of line managers turning down black applicants sent to them by personnel. The reasons for rejection given freely to personnel managers were 'we have enough of them already—don't send us any more' or 'we don't want any of them in our department'.

This type of incident presents a personnel manager with a real dilemma. On the one hand, he is charged with the responsibility of objectively finding good people for the organization but on the other he needs to bear in mind the demands made by his client, the line manager. The Race Relations Act should prove a good ally to any personnel manager pinned on the horns of this dilemma. Line managers must be made aware of the possible repercussions, both personal and organizational, of racial discrimination but personnel managers will want to convey this kind of information without antagonizing or alienating any particular line manager. In the absence of any company policy on race relations, referring to the law would seem a good way of achieving this.

Evaluation

Few of the companies in our sample did any systematic evaluation of their selection methods or criteria. Even fewer had reviewed their recruitment and selection processes with a view to identifying practices which might result in unfair indirect discrimination. The organizations which did most on evaluation tended to be those with the more systematic selection procedures. Ironically it would seem that, where racial discrimination is concerned, these are the organizations which need to do less on evaluation because the more informal the selection, the more vulnerable it is to prejudice. Because of the insidious (but sometimes completely unintentional) way in which bias can enter into selection, all organizations would be wise to satisfy themselves that their own means of finding and choosing employees is free of racial discrimination.

Promotion and transfer

Our survey of organizations revealed a similar picture for the distribution of ethnic minorities in employment to that found in almost all other studies. In simple terms, the majority of black workers were concentrated in low-grade low-status jobs. Whereas some people would say that, based on the history of immigration, this is only to be expected, the fact that so few of these workers get promoted into more responsible jobs is not so easily explained away. We encountered several instances where the supervisor was the only white employee in a particular department or function. Few of the managers in organizations where this was so had given serious thought or done any thorough analysis of why none of the black shop-floor workers had been made up to the supervisor level as would normally have happened. We were offered a number of notional explanations:

'They are not good enough.'

'They have not been here long enough and don't have the necessary experience.'

'They have no confidence in themselves and they are frightened of the tests usually because they can't read or write well enough.'

'Being promoted means being alienated.'

A more considered look at some of these explanations was quite revealing. On the two occasions when we were told that the ethnic minorities were not good enough to be supervisors, we had already been told that 'they are some of our best workers'. This may not be as contradictory as it sounds for the abilities needed by a supervisor are not necessarily the same as those possessed by a good shop-floor worker. However, in these same situations the black workers had not become job instructors or shop stewards either. Neither of these positions demands exactly the same personal capabilities or attitudes as those needed in the good supervisor, so it does seem as if some general restraint on movement out from the basic level of employment was operating in the case of ethnic minorities.

The question of experience was indeed a necessary factor for promotion in most cases but often the organizations concerned had been employing substantial numbers of immigrants for 10 to 20 years. The explanations that alluded to a reluctance on the part of the black workers themselves to seek promotion, due to 'promotion meaning alienation', did appear to have validity. We recorded a number of examples of organizations unsuccessfully trying to persuade individuals or groups to train or apply for supervisory jobs. In the two cases where black workers had agreed to become supervisors both had resulted in failure, one worker returning to the shop floor and one leaving the organization. These failures were said to have nothing to do with change in earning potential. They were caused by an inability to transcend attitudinal barriers.

Many black workers are known to be purely instrumental in their approach to work. They do not go through formal machinery like grievance procedures as much as their white workmates nor do they play their full part in the informal parts of organizational life, like joining in the annual works outing. In the case of Asian immigrants, this may be explained by the fact that for some of them their principal point of reference is still their country of origin. They are working in a British organization largely because of the money they can earn, some of which will be sent to support relatives back home. This approach to working life is sometimes welcomed by management, who feel these workers do a good job and do it without causing as many problems as others do. Black worker and management therefore come to have an expectation of each other and each then adopts a tacitly agreed role. In these circumstances, therefore, there is little wonder that the idea of promotion for this 'instrumental' worker never enters the minds of individuals in either group.

This sort of attitudinal barrier can also apply for black workers born and raised in this country. If a youngster grows up in a decaying environment, lives in inferior housing, attends poorer, overcrowded schools and constantly feels himself the subject of unfair discrimination, it should surprise no-one that he is antagonistic or at best unsympathetic towards the 'establishment' elements in society. A recent major publicity campaign aimed at recruiting black policemen failed badly. This was said to be due in part to the 'them and us' attitudes caused through social deprivation. This may apply equally to the industrial setting and could well be at least a partial explanation of this high group loyalty and the reluctance of black workers to leave the 'us' and join the 'them'. One Asian was in fact said to have explained his refusal to accept promotion with the words 'It's all right for you but I have to live with them'.

Although it is not within the power of individual managers to change the social conditions which produce these attitudes, a manager may well see advantages to be gained by overcoming their effects within his own situation. It has already been argued that intense 'them and us' perceptions can be extremely harmful to productivity and although the highly instrumental approach on the part of workers is often believed to make for an easier life for managers, it may be that this is damaging to the organization as a whole. Overcoming these attitudinal barriers will not be easy and will usually require positive or 'affirmative action' programmes. This sort of programme, which is discussed in more detail later, can also be used to dispel any lacking of confidence or fear of tests. Help can be offered to people in preparing for supervisory positions.

Apart from the explanations considered so far there is also the factor that the black worker's lack of movement out of basic grades in employment can be due to racial discrimination. Organizations will therefore need to look at the way they tend to promote people so as to identify any areas where unfair discrimination may be taking place. The means of advertising vacancies, the nature of any tests, the criteria used in arriving at decisions will all need to be reviewed.

One further possibility is, as a manager put it, that 'the white workers just would not stand for having a black supervisor over them'. We would suggest that in many cases, this is not so. Even if such racial prejudice is in evidence, managers need only to act in exactly the same way as they would in any other situation where a part of the organization was doing something which was both unlawful and against the best interests of the organization as a whole. Resolving such difficulties is very much a part of management and well-managed organizations will find solutions that are appropriate to their own situations.

Clustering

Another facet of the distribution of ethnic minorities in employment is that they may often be found concentrated in particular departments, functions or shifts. This 'clustering' was said to have both advantages and disadvantages.

Working with others of the same racial origin is often preferred by ethnic minorities. They feel that this gives them higher levels of security and satisfaction at work. They can work with the people they live near and this reduces the chances of their suffering the indignity and anxiety brought by racial discrimination. Gathering together in particular departments or shifts may also be sought because of economic considerations or domestic convenience.

Certain managers appear happy to see this clustering occur. If the black workers seemed happy and caused few problems, this usually meant that there were fewer difficulties for the managers to deal with. Allowing clusters to form also made it easier to recruit workers for unpleasant jobs or unsocial working hours. In some instances, this meant that the workforce was multiracial in name only, because each functional area was relatively homogeneous where race was concerned. This aspect also pleased some managers as they believed it reduced the possibility of their having to deal with racial conflict.

Other managers were very much against clustering. Several objected on principle, believing that ultimately the quality of human relations within the organization, which subtly but quite profoundly influenced effectiveness, could only be harmed by accepting racial segregation in the enterprise. They believed that such separation, far from preventing racial conflict, would inexorably lead to confrontations. Several managers were against clustering for immediate operational reasons. They believed groups of black workers tended to be more cohesive and acted in concert more often than their white counterparts. This meant they might be more likely to hold the company to ransom, so for reasons of control this clustering should be discouraged. Homogeneous racial groups could also make it difficult for the company to recruit, promote or transfer on merit. We heard of one example where a company had to close down a part of its operation because of this problem.

Overall, most managers were against clustering. Some managements appeared to operate a policy of 'no clustering' in a much more authoritarian way than they implemented other policies. It seemed, as a consequence, that some black applicants and employees might be treated unfairly. It would be inappropriate to make sweeping judgements on the advantages or otherwise of clustering. This will differ from situation to situation. Organizations will need to make up their own minds but they should ensure, first, that whatever policy is decided upon does not bring them into conflict with the law and, secondly, that their actions are likely to foster racial harmony.

Induction and training

Induction

Despite the fact that several managers felt that there was a need for it, none of the organizations included in our study had made special arrangements for the induction of ethnic minorities into their employment. Particularly in the case of Asians, it appeared that workers often sat through the induction programme in an uninterested manner, having little contact with anyone except fellow Asians. These new employees rarely asked questions and several managers said it was clear that the organization's standard induction programmes were less effective for these ethnic minorities. It appeared that the black workers often waited for the induction they would get from black workmates already employed by the firm.

The basic purposes of induction are to introduce new employees to the organization and to their immediate working environment. Good induction will mean that workers are more speedily assimilated and reach required levels of productivity in a shorter time. It starts them off on the right lines as far as the company is concerned and helps prevent problems that might otherwise arise from random or ill-prepared entry to the organization. A good induction programme will also help to minimize labour turnover. It seems that for many black workers the basic aims of induction are often not fulfilled as well as for other new employees. Special adaptation or extension of the normal induction programme is therefore called for in some instances. Those managers who agreed with this but did nothing felt that to set up special arrangements just for black recruits would be seen as a favouring of a particular group. This could generate resentment and be counter-productive. Even if this were so, it would not be hard for a company to make a good case to justify special measures. First, the company could collect evidence to show that the general induction scheme was working less well for a particular group and so demonstrate a need. Secondly, it could explain that the purpose of induction was to bring everyone up to a basic level of preparedness for taking up jobs in the organization. If any new recruits for some reason (being born and schooled overseas or being generally disadvantaged in society) were further away from this basic level of preparedness than the average recruit, in the interests of all concerned companies need to do more to bring them up to the necessary standard.

The distorted impressions of managers and management held by some Asians is one example of a potentially harmful misconception of the sort that could be improved through an appropriate induction programme. We asked managers what they believed their Asian employees would say about the organization's management. The reply given by one manager 'Who cares', shows that he had little appreciation of the damage that misinformation and misconception can cause.

We believe that systematic evaluation of induction programmes would show the value of amending them for particular groups of new employees. In our study we found regrettably little evidence of the sort of monitoring and evaluation of induction programmes which would reveal their relative efficacy.

The need for special induction is usually associated with those who were born overseas and spent most of their formative years in a very different cultural setting from that of Britain. We saw indications that adapting induction programmes might also pay dividends with those born in Britain but who were clearly disadvantaged. As we note later, some black workers are never as fully integrated into the organization as other workers. A thorough but flexible approach to induction could show the whole workforce that the organization truly wished to give opportunities to all with the talent and energy to make use of them. This will go a long way to securing the involvement of disadvantaged groups and might also contribute to getting a better industrial relations climate in general.

Becoming skilled

One of the main reasons given for the heavy concentration of black workers in lower grade jobs was that they were themselves reluctant to undertake training for more skilled jobs. Some explanations have already been given for this reported reticence of black workers to make any move away from the security of their closest reference group. One of these explanations concerned the fear or lack of confidence associated with anything which required qualifying, being tested, or showing good literacy and numeracy. This was said to apply particularly in the case of training and was most pronounced in the case of apprenticeships. Thus it was not surprising that we found a disproportionately low number of young black people in apprenticeship schemes in the organizations covered by our survey. Racial prejudice must be included in any explanation of why ethnic minorities are under-represented in apprenticeship schemes. In one company which did have a few black apprentices the personnel manager, at our request, called outside the room to ask a member of his department exactly how many black apprentices the organization had on its books. The reply from this unseen subordinate was 'too bloody many!'

There are some signs which suggest that more black school leavers are moving into apprenticeships. This may be due to some extent to the increasing number of them, born and educated in Britain, who are leaving school with British educational qualifications. It may also be due in part to the difficulty employers in some industries seem to have in persuading school leavers to take apprenticeships. The Training Opportunities Scheme (TOPS) run by the Training Services Agency should also mean that more adult black workers can become skilled. Thus there are hopeful signs but the experience of our study leads us to believe that organizations could do more to help black workers train for more skilled jobs. One manufacturing company set in an area with a high proportion of black people in the working population provides a good example of what can be done. This company decided not to use academic qualifications exclusively for selecting entrants to its craft apprenticeship scheme. Instead some other criteria such as motivation to learn and manual dexterity were used. As a result of this method of selection, several black school leavers without O levels or CSEs were taken on to a pre-apprenticeship course. All these black youngsters completed the course and went on to the apprenticeship scheme, where they were said to be performing admirably.

Language training

A recent major survey revealed that around 40 per cent of Asian men and 60 per cent of Asian women speak English only slightly or not at all.[33] This problem is not confined to those of Asian origin. It applies to several other ethnic minority groups with mother tongues other than English. It also applies to some black people who although brought up to speak English, have a highly distinctive vocabulary and dialect. All these people will experience some difficulty in communicating solely in English with workers or managers of different origins. The effectiveness of the organization, which may well have a language of its own, will undoubtedly suffer because of the existence of these shortcomings in language proficiency.

Some managers did not accept that their organizations had any need to provide work-related language training, let alone training for social use. These managers believed that if language training of any kind was needed, it should be provided by local authorities in schools or colleges during the evenings or other times when workers were free. A few of the managers we consulted went so far as to suggest that their companies would get little or no benefit from sponsoring language training. As these were the same managers who said that their organizations would be insisting on good spoken English as an essential requirement in the selection of new recruits, their own views appear to conflict. If it is in the interests of the organization only to take on people who speak English well, this must mean that the organization could also gain by training those of its existing employees who do not speak English to this standard. Companies who do decide that it is right in principal that they should provide language training will need to identify the most cost effective way to proceed. Persuading a local educational institution to provide courses in the evenings may well be the cheapest method but all the evidence points to language teaching at the workplace as the most effective way of language training. This is because:

1 Shift patterns, long working hours and family commitments prevent many workers from attending evening classes
   It is only through on-site training that the majority of them can be reached; for example, 31 per cent of Asian and West Indian employees work shifts compared with 15 per cent of the white population
2 It is at the place of work that black workers are most likely to be in regular contact with those whose mother tongue is English
3 Effective language *learning* means *using* that language successfully. Language classes must be backed up with encouragement and support from English speakers. By involving them, the whole system of communications on the shopfloor can be modified[34]

Providing irrefutable evidence of the cost benefit of language training is practically impossible. As with any training of this kind, it is hard to attribute specific effects to particular causes. The effectiveness of language training may also differ from situation to situation and from person to person. Hence it is not surprising that there have been relatively few studies done on the evaluation of language training. One of the few such evaluations which have been carried out and published[35] was done by staff of the Rubber and Plastics Processing Industrial Training Board.

In conjunction with an organization which has since developed and has become the Government-sponsored National Centre for Industrial Language Training, a language training course for Asian immigrants was developed. This course was specifically produced for Indian women working in an assembly room of a small plastics firm employing around 350 people. A thorough investigation of the work of the women in this department was carried out initially, giving particular attention to the views of first line supervisors on problems as they saw them. The course tutors actually worked in the department so that they could become familiar with jargon and social activity patterns. From this work it became evident that a language course likely to benefit the company should aim to:

1 Reduce the level of supervision required for non-English speakers
2 Reduce the use of interpreters
3 Improve the flexibility of the workforce, that is, the ability to become proficient at more of the jobs in the department through creating a greater understanding of job instruction.[36]

A course programme was designed to meet these aims. This had a target of 60 hours, to be run for one hour per day for 12 weeks. The lesson time of one hour was considered to be the best length. It was thought that learning proficiency would fall sharply if lessons were longer and took place less frequently. It was also agreed that lessons should take place in the first hour of the day so that the trainees would not have to interrupt their work and run the risk of damage to unattended work in progress.

The course consisted of six main sections each lasting approximately 10 hours (two weeks):

1 Building confidence, establishing teaching methods, remedial grammar
2 Set language forms at work, language product and process faults, simple social conversations
3 Responding to more complicated situations, measurement and accuracy
4 All about the factory

5 Initiating communication
6 Extension and revision.[37]

At the end of the course, an assessment was made of how far the original objectives of the course had been met. The evaluation was based on evidence from three sources: course tutors, supervisors and measurable factors within the department concerned. All three sources indicated that the course had been successful. In terms of the quantitative factors such as output productivity and quality control taken overall, these were definitely improved. For example, there was a 7 per cent increase in productivity for the group. As the new standards were seen to be substantially maintained (checks were made several months after the close of the programme), these gains were assumed to be real.

The instigators of the programme concluded that:

> We thought we had found a reasonably successful solution to a problem which, insofar as it had been tackled, had not been solved. Of course, there were many snags still and the teachers could see a number of improvements which could be made but we felt in no doubt that, for certain situations, we had found a practical means of increasing the efficiency of these overseas workers and of enriching their lives.*[38]

In our study, we found very few instances of language training being given serious consideration. In the two

*All the information given here about the language training course comes from an article by J W Leppard and M Kaufman, of the Rubber and Plastics Processing Industry Training Board. The entire article is well worth reading for those managers considering the idea of setting up language training courses. An address for the National Centre for Industrial Language Training with some further information is given in Appendix Three

cases where some sort of language training was provided, the outcome could not be described as totally successful. The drop-out rate and general lack of interest of the black workers concerned was the main reason for this. A question is therefore raised against the efficacy of doing language training where workers wish to adhere strongly to an instrumental approach to work and where, in all other matters except language, management also welcomes this approach. If the employee is happy with his competence in speaking English and regards language training as an unnecessary imposition, then neither he nor the company is likely to gain much even if he does complete the course. This point serves to illustrate the importance of discussing the question of language training with those concerned before any decision is made. If the workers can be convinced of the benefits that can undoubtedly accrue to both individual and organization from a well-administered language training course, the outcome is much more likely to be successful.

Industrial relations

Conflict in organizations

It is inevitable that conflict will occur between people within organizations. Clashes between people at work can be of different kinds and on different levels. For example, the argument between two operatives who work the same machine but on different shifts, each blaming the other for its malfunctioning, is different from the dispute shown in collective bargaining between management and union, yet both are forms of industrial conflict.

The term industrial conflict is now almost exclusively associated with management versus union confrontations and this is the area where most 'industrial relations' attention is focused. This is regrettable to say the least because, taken cumulatively over any period, the damage done by unresolved conflict (through high labour turnover, absenteeism, reduced productivity and poor quality work) can be far more costly than an official strike. Inept management may well suffer from both, as a withdrawal of labour is only the most extreme manifestation of discontent (representing withdrawals of commitment and enthusiasm). These other, less obvious manifestations of conflict will often therefore take place as precursors to a strike.

Management has a responsibility to handle and cope with conflict in the organization. Managerial strategies of neglect or authoritarianism when faced with disagreements of any kind may sometimes be successful, but in most cases we believe they will be inadequate. Managers in the modern organization increasingly need to possess the skills associated with resolving or coping with conflict. This will mean that for each situation they can find an appropriate process which will enable the people concerned to negotiate an agreed settlement and, further, a settlement which on balance also serves the interests of the whole organization.

There is no doubt that conflict regularly occurs between people of different races in their place of work. The extent to which this constitutes a racial problem, in the sense that it is caused by differences in ethnic origin, seems difficult to decide. We were told of many 'racial incidents' which started off as simple differences of opinion on work matters. This might be the sort of problem which regularly occurs between employees whatever their race, for instance, arguments between production and maintenance workers. These incidents only took on racial overtones when tempers got frayed. It seems as well to remember that calling someone a black so-and-so at the end of a heated exchange may or may not be due to underlying racial tension.

The following paragraphs itemize the principal race relations problems occurring in multi-racial workforces as described by managers. In presenting this information, we are aware that several of the problems are specific to particular groups of immigrants and that, according to informed opinion, they will soon be problems of the past. Nevertheless, we feel it right to include them for the benefit of readers who may still encounter such difficulties. We also include them because, though being obvious and extreme examples, they are indicative of the attitudinal and behavioural problems which will still need to be tackled in the years immediately ahead.

Attitudes and behaviour

The mistaken beliefs which were refuted with facts in Part I may be myths but they can be real enough in effect. Irrationally attaching blame to ethnic minorities for all kinds of social and economic ills affects the attitudes of the minority groups themselves and can also cause detrimental changes in the behaviour of the rest of the community.

Most people in our society know little of ethnic minorities and have little contact with them, so it is easy for mutual distrust to grow. This lack of acquaintance is revealed in the heavy stereotyping which is applied to particular racial groups. In the organizations we visited, black workers were variously described as unhygienic, lazy, aggressive, money mad and of low intelligence. Although any individual member of a particular race may possess one or more of these undesirable traits, it is illogical to make such sweeping generalizations about the race as a whole.

The tendency of managers to regard collections of ethnic minority workers as a single entity with one will, one mind and one temperament may also be a result of this lack of understanding. This tendency may account for the contention held by some managers that groups of black workers go back on their word more often than other workers. Managers often deal with black workers through a spokesman who may or may not have any official standing; this spokesman is often picked for his command of English and not for his possession of any leadership role. This means that any agreement or understanding he arrives at with management will often be gone back upon or amended after it has been discussed by the entire group.

We heard little of some of the well-known anecdotes about eating, spitting, washing feet in handbasins and similar personal habits. Two recent instances of problems over the usage of lavatories by Asians were described to us. In each case, the companies concerned thought of putting in special equipment. One company, without consulting union or workers, decided to go ahead and two 'Asian toilets' were installed. This was said to cause no problems but there had been some reluctance to use the facilities because, it was claimed, of the anxiety that was generated by being seen to be different. The other company discussed its intentions with workers' representatives, including Asians. It was clear that a majority were against the provision of special facilities. The company was surprised to find that following its consultation with workers' representatives, no further complaints of this kind were made. One manager attributed this to the simple fact that the company had shown its intention to remedy the difficulty.

In almost all of the organizations we visited, managers reported difficulties about requests for extended leave to visit relatives back home. Because of the frequency of such requests, and the amount of abuse when concessions were made, most of the companies took a hard line on extended leave. Some were reluctant to make this concession at all while others had policies which were rigidly observed. In a few of these policies, accumulation of holidays was allowed but all included a strict upper limit to the amount of leave allowed. Typically, requests for extended leave would involve the following procedure. The employee concerned would usually make his request to a supervisor who would refer it to the personnel department, which would check the dates involved, the length and nature of service of the employee, the extent to which this would inconvenience line management and reasons given for the request. An interview with the employee would invariably take place. If the company decided that it should grant extended leave, the employee was usually informed officially by letter. This letter would specify the dates concerned and would indicate that if the employee did not return by the agreed date, his name would be taken off the company's books. This point is of some importance as re-entry to the country can be prolonged without proper details of employment. The employee would be asked to reply to this letter before departure, indicating his intention to return as agreed. Despite this extensive procedure, many managers claimed that they had problems with employees who went beyond the agreed extent of leave. It was said to be quite common for the company to receive telegrams giving reasons for failure to return. Managers found it hard to decide whether these were genuine since the practice occurred so often with particular racial groups. In many instances, managers claimed they had to be authoritarian otherwise the situation would get out of hand.

This need for a firm hand was also said to apply to requests for time off to pray. Muslims must pray several times a day and whereas most of them manage to fit this requirement into their normal work routine, some workers insist they need to have special breaks. While such a request presents no problems in some situations, in many others managers feel they have to refuse because of the disruptions it would cause to production and to fellow-workers. A further issue associated with religion concerns holy festivals. In some instances, members of a certain religion feel they should not or could not work on these days. A few managers appeared to be tolerant on this issue and one organization with a large proportion of a particular religious group in its workforce closed the works annually on an important day coinciding with a religious festival. As the personnel manager said, 'Many of them would holiday anyway and if they had asked for time off and we had refused, we would end up having to discipline them. No-one wants that.'

This type of issue (extended leave, time for prayers and religious festivals) can be perplexing for managers. Some resent these problems being introduced into their lives. They feel that these difficulties are being caused unnecessarily by people who refuse to give up an 'alien way of life'. Most managers take a different view. They want to do all they can to grant the requests of the ethnic minorities but only insofar as their principal task of running the business is not affected. They believe that the effectiveness of the organization would undoubtedly suffer from a freer approach. These managers are also worried about the consequence of allowing irregular breaks for prayers, or giving greatly extended leave allowance, where the rest of the workforce is concerned. If everyone demanded similar concessions, the enterprise might become unmanageable.

The strategy adopted by many managers is to devise policies and procedures and then to implement them to the letter. The information gathered from managers in our study suggests that formalizing policies on these questions is advisable in most instances. It appeared that in some cases the policies, by being excessively stringent, were more likely to cause problems than to solve them. A policy of 'no extended leave until five years service' is likely to be a constant irritant. Similarly 'no concessions on religious holidays' may be very provocative. On the other hand, having a completely free approach may bring problems too. If four out of 10 operatives on a shift all decide to go overseas for a long spell at the same time, the organization will suffer heavily. Similarly, if a request is granted in one case, it sets a precedent which is hard to deny to someone who makes the same request but in very different circumstances. The only answer is to find a policy which is thought to be fair to both individual and organization. This may be easier to say than to do but once such a policy is agreed, it can be communicated and explained fully to all employees and to all future recruits. With all policies, when an exceptional case arises, managers will need to show a degree of flexibility if the issue in question is to be satisfactorily settled.

Ethnic minorities and unions

We found only two instances of black workers acting as shop stewards in the companies we visited. Although several managers said that there had been black shop stewards in their organizations in previous years, there was no doubt that ethnic minority union representatives tended to be relatively rare. Managers gave a number of explanations for this. Prejudice was felt to play a part but the minority group's own lack of interest in union matters was believed to be the principal reason. In several cases it was claimed that black workers viewed their union cards like the old National Insurance cards. They were something workers had to have if they were to be 'left alone to work in peace'.

Although we did find a few instances where whole groups of black workers were said to be good union members, in general they did seem to be more apathetic towards the unions. Ethnic minority groups appeared to consider that unions had little relevance for them and that they were more the preserve of white workers. Consequently these groups believed that they were expected not to involve themselves in union matters even though from time to time attempts were made to persuade them otherwise. When workers have such attitudes, the union cannot be an effective means of communicating or representing their interests and alternative mechanisms to those which apply for white union members may be sought. There are two obvious alternatives: first, the individual worker (or group of workers) may take it upon himself to talk to management on his own behalf; secondly, an alternative agency from outside the organization can be used. To take the first course of action means that the complainant feels sufficiently confident of his ability to represent himself and to influence management favourably. This will clearly not always be so but we did hear of several instances where this alternative to using a union was taken. We were told of individual black 'troublemakers' who 'pestered' managers with their grievances. Managers were often annoyed by this refusal to follow normal procedure but in some circumstances they realized that the only effective way to resolve a dispute was by adapting usual procedures. We heard of one case where a group of workers stopped working, sat down on the floor and refused to let the union speak to management on their behalf. Eventually, the management talked directly to the whole minority group. A blackboard was brought into the room and all the group's grievances were recorded down one half of the blackboard. Each grievance was discussed in turn and an agreed management action was negotiated and written up alongside the appropriate issue. A management representative then signed the board and the whole 'agreement' was typed and signed again. By following this procedure, the dispute was brought to an end and the employees resumed work.

Most managers appeared to be strongly against the idea of outside agencies representing workers. Nevertheless, we did encounter cases where such agencies did become involved. Some company disciplinary procedures allow a worker facing a complaint to get a friend to speak on his behalf. Although in most instances this role is played by the shop steward it appears that members of ethnic minority groups sometimes choose to have as their 'friend' a representative of an ethnic minority association or society. Presumably they do this because they believe that their case will be better supported by this association than by their union.

Dealing with any alternative to a recognized union is likely to be a sensitive matter for management. The unions concerned may see it as dangerously usurping their role and as something sufficiently important to make into a major issue. At the same time, management has to find a way of resolving disputes and, if a shop steward or union is not accepted as a representative of the aggrieved workers, a solution still has to be found. We were given a few examples of managers seeking alternatives to the normal means of negotiating with workers. In one well-known case, the management of an organization employing Muslim workers approached the local Mosque leaders and asked for their help in resolving the dispute.

Few people believe that special or separate arrangements for any section of the workforce are desirable or advisable. They should be considered only as a last resort. Nevertheless, if for any reason normal procedures prove to be insufficient, managers will need to adapt their approach to suit the needs of the situation. Flexibility is the hallmark of good management.

Policies and practice

The set of issues we have described is far from being a complete list and many more may be found in the literature on different aspects of race relations in employment (a short reading list is provided in Appendix Four). But they provide an up to date sample of areas where special efforts may have to be made if multi-racial workforces are to be managed more effectively and justly.

Taking action to combat racial discrimination and disadvantage will often centre on a company policy. Some people are against the formulation and publication of these so-called equal opportunity policies (which usually proscribe discrimination on grounds of sex, race, creed and colour). They say that experience has shown there is very little positive correlation (and in some cases a negative correlation) between such policies and practice. Examples are often quoted of particular organizations which have had policies for years but have done little in practice. We believe that despite these experiences there is a strong case in favour of organizations having race relations policies. In the first place, a declaration of intent on the elimination of discrimination gives an official 'line' to which many employees will automatically adhere. In one Midlands factory a recruitment officer told us that, in accordance with company policy, the recruitment and selection process was continually checked for evidence of any discrimination.

He also said 'This company does not tolerate racial discrimination and I do everything I can to support that but what I do in my own time is my own business.' This recruitment officer told us that although he got on well with the company's black employees, he always curtly refused if they invited him to their homes or sought any kind of social meeting outside work. To use this man's own words, 'I'm prejudiced but the company isn't'.

A policy is also of great importance for any industrial tribunal cases or other complaints. An organization is liable for any discriminatory acts carried out by its agents or employees in the course of their employment, unless the organization can prove it took all reasonable practicable steps to prevent such acts occurring. A policy will help prevent discrimination and will also show that the organization has attempted to proscribe such behaviour if any employee should cause a complaint to be made against the company.

Policies seem especially necessary when the organization is decentralized or where there is an extended hierarchy; here, managers in particular locations may have considerable autonomy. A policy will provide them with guildelines and will ensure that they act in keeping with the values laid down by the organization. An example of the practical use of a policy was given to us by a personnel manager who had suspected for some time a senior line manager was condoning and practising racial discrimination; he was able to get this manager to stop such practices by reference to the company policy. This personnel manager believed that without the policy it would have been impossible for him to have influenced the line manager in this way.

Jointly agreed

One of the principal criticisms of policies, that they are effective in the boardroom only, will be less likely to apply if any policy is generated or agreed with representatives of the workforce. This will mean that in most cases the advice and assistance of the appropritate trade unions will need to be sought. Invitations to trade unions to become involved in policy formulation on race may not always be accepted. We met two instances where the trade union representatives were strongly against management action to eliminate racial discrimination and disadvantage. In both cases management had indicated its intention to continue the attempt to end discrimination. As we have already reported, we also met one example of a union devising its own policy and programme because of the inactivity of the organization's management.

The TUC is attempting to provide a lead for its members on race relations. A national rally on this subject was recently held. The Congress has issued a Model Equal Opportunities Clause and has recommended that it should be written into all relevant agreements with employees. Amongst a number of other activities, the TUC is also introducing a training programme on race relations into the standard shop steward training package. It is to be hoped that these TUC initiatives will mean a greater interest in combating discrimination and disadvantage on the part of trade union representatives, and that this will be a spur and an aid to management.

Managers will have to make up their own minds on whether it is feasible to invite trade union cooperation in this area. There can be no doubt that the policy is likely to be more meaningful and effective if a wide range of worker representatives participate in creating it. Nevertheless, if for any reason such participation is impossible, management might at least seek the agreement of trade unions on an equal opportunities policy. The following example is a joint agreement drawn up for a company in North London—the agreement is based very largely on the TUCs model clause.

COMPANY TITLE
ADDRESS

UNION TITLE
ADDRESS

EQUAL OPPORTUNITIES AGREEMENT

Both parties to this Agreement are committed to the development of positive policies to promote equal opportunity in employment regardless of workers' sex, marital status, creed, colour, race or ethnic origins. This principle will apply in respect of all conditions of work, including pay, hours of work, holiday entitlement, overtime and shiftwork, work allocation, guaranteed earnings, sick pay, pensions, recruitment, training, promotion and redundancy.

Management undertakes to direct the attention of all eligible employees to opportunities for training and promotion and to inform all employees of the Agreement on equal opportunity.

Both parties agree to regularly review, through the present negotiating machinery, the operation of this equal opportunity policy.

Should an employee consider that he or she is suffering from unequal treatment on the grounds of sex, marital status, creed, colour, race or ethnic origins, he or she may make a complaint which will be dealt with through the agreed procedures for dealing with grievances.

SIGNED
Company Managing Director
Union Area Organizer

Kinds of policy

Basically an organization may decide to have one of two types of policy on race. It can opt for non-discrimination or it can choose an affirmative action policy. Non-discrimination policies simply give notice that the company will obey the law and will not tolerate discrimination. Programmes of action based on such policies attempt to ensure that none of the organization's practices or procedures discriminate against ethnic minorities. Affirmative action, on the other hand, is meant to reduce the disadvantage faced by ethnic minorities in addition to eliminating discrimination. For example, the organization's requirements for entry into skills training may give equal opportunity in the sense that they are the same for everyone. Even so, fewer black employees may apply for and go on to do these schemes because of language difficulties, lack of confidence and so on. In an affirmative action programme, the company will provide assistance and general encouragement to black workers so that more of them will be able to apply for skills training. Consequently, in terms of removing disadvantage, affirmative action is likely to be much more effective.

The main objection to affirmative action is that it may be seen as putting the black worker in a privileged position. It is claimed that other workers may deeply resent this 'favouritism' and race relations could in fact be more harmed than improved. Similarly, by over-emphasizing ethnicity, some problems which were not essentially racial in origin might become so. If managers have good reason to believe that this is a possibility, it becomes even more important that representatives of all interested parties should be involved in the organization's consideration and eventual decision as to what policy should be adopted.

Implementation

The precise nature of the policy which is eventually

arrived at will be specific to the organization, thus it is unrealistic to be too prescriptive. Irrespective of the policy chosen the following points, if followed, should nevertheless enable it to have an impactful and beneficial outcome.

1 The policy should be clearly and simply written. If at all possible, it should be formulated in conjunction with the representatives of all major interest groups in the organization

2 It should be publicly endorsed by senior management with, when feasible, the agreement of all unions and staff associations concerned

3 It should be efficiently and extensively communicated to all employees and should be made evident through all media associated with the organization
The Bank of California's instructions on the dissemination of its affirmative action programme is a useful example:
   i) Officers and employees will be informed of the Bank's written statement of policy by:
      (a) Distribution of policy statement to all management personnel with responsibility for implementation and administration of policy
      (b) Description of policy by publication or reference in all issues or re-issues of employee handbooks
      (c) Communication of policy, when appropriate, through news stories or other articles in Bank publications
      (d) Detailed discussions at management conferences such as supervisory meetings
      (e) Discussion in the orientation program for new employees in all departments and at all levels.
   ii) Employment advertisements will contain assurance of equal employment opportunity

iii) All employment and recruiting sources where jobs are listed by the Bank will be informed of our policy, both verbally and in writing

iv) Notices will be posted on Bulletin Boards in locations where applicants are interviewed.[39]

4 An individual, perhaps assisted by a committee representing the pluralism of interests in the organization, should be made responsible for supervising and monitoring the policy and for reporting back to the board at regular intervals

The policy should be frequently reviewed on the basis of these reports

5 The policy should be more than a simple declaration of intent to develop equal opportunity. It should make specific reference to how it will be put into action on, for example Communication and consultation

Records and monitoring
Recruitment and selection
Induction, training and development
Promotion and transfer
Industrial relations.

6 The policy should be introduced into the organization in an appropriate manner. This may mean that in some instances the policy may be implemented sequentially through different levels or functions of the organization

7 If the organization is made up of different units or locations, the policy formed at the centre should be amended at each location or unit. These amended policies should be returned to the centre for approval.

Important questions to ask

The precise nature of the policies chosen by an organization will depend on its existing situation. For this reason, it is inappropriate to suggest that all organizations should pursue any particular policy. We have already discussed some of the principal issues which we encountered. Organizations will want to check if these or other potentially disruptive issues apply in their own case and the following list[40] of questions may help managers to review their own spheres of control. A review of this kind might be the starting point of affirmative action; it will highlight where action is most needed or where it would be most beneficial. Alternatively, the list might provide the basis for reviewing and monitoring in a non-discrimination approach.

Recruitment and selection

1 What are the major ethnic minority groups in the local labour market?
  Approximately, what proportion of the total working population do these groups represent?
  What are the corresponding figures for the organization?
  Is there any evidence to suggest that black workers tend not to apply for jobs with the organization?
2 What means of advertising vacancies and channels

for recruiting does the organization tend to use? Do these tend to favour any section of the community?

3 In selection are all the criteria used clearly relevant to the requirements of the job?
   Are they derived systematically?
   Does the organization ask for minimum standards of reading, writing or speaking English?
   How are these standards assessed?
   Does the application form need re-designing?
   If criteria are used which are not job-related, do they operate unfairly to the disadvantage of ethnic minorities?
   Do the criteria for selection include any unnecessary age or experience bias?
   If the criteria are operating unfairly, how can they be changed?
4 Does the selection procedure have any in-built bias?
   Is this procedure evaluated?
   How?
   How often?
5 Are tests used?
   Have they been checked for cultural bias?
   How are qualifications and experience gained overseas assessed?
6 Are records kept of all inquiries, applicants and interviews with reasons for rejection or acceptance?
   Do these include a record of the race, colour or country of birth of applicant?
7 Are the people responsible for recruitment and selection aware of the law and of any company policy on racial discrimination?

Promotion and transfer

1 Have segregated situations developed (shifts, sections or departments staffed entirely or mostly by workers

of a particular race or colour)?
Why is this so?

2 Are all vacancies fully advertised to everyone in the organization?
Is there any evidence that black employees receive inadequate notification of opportunities and the ability, qualifications and experience needed?

3 Is there any evidence that higher standards are required of black employees than of others in any part of the organization for any particular type of job?

4 Do all employees in the organization have their performance reviewed periodically to ensure that those with ability for promotion are identified and that training needs are highlighted and acted upon?

5 Have qualified black employees been denied access to supervisory, managerial, technical or administrative positions or posts carrying higher pay and/or status in any part of the company?
Do the criteria for promotion include any non job-related factors?
Do these discriminate against ethnic minorities?

6 How many supervisors are members of ethnic minority groups?
Are these groups under-represented in supervisory grades of employment?
If so, why is this so?

7 Are tests used in selecting supervisors?
Do these disadvantage or discourage workers from ethnic minority groups?

8 Is training for supervision given?

9 Do all those responsible for promotion or placement know the organization's policy on equal opportunity?
Are they aware of the relevant aspects of the Race Relations Act 1976?

Induction and training

1 Is induction given?
  Is this evaluated?
  Are there any indications that the induction programme is less effective in the case of ethnic minority groups?
2 Are details of all training opportunities fully communicated to all employees?
  Do members of ethnic minority groups tend not to take advantage of the opportunities as much as the rest of the workforce?
  Why is this so?
3 Are the requirements for skills training discriminating against or disadvantaging members of ethnic minority groups?
  If so, can they be justified?
4 Is language training necessary?

Industrial relations

1 Do members of ethnic minority groups tend to use existing procedures (for example, complaints procedures) less than other workers?
  Why is this so?
2 Are there any issues which are a potential source of conflict between different ethnic groups?
  Is there any need for the organization to take special measures on the integration of different racial groups?
  Is there any evidence of stereotyping: are recruitment, training or promotion decisions based on pre-conceived notions of the capabilities or other characteristics of particular groups?
  Are members of particular groups directed into or excluded from particular jobs in the organization on the basis of untested assumptions about them as members of that group rather than as individuals?

3 Does the company have any policies and procedures on such matters as extended leave, time off for prayers or religious holidays etc?
Are these felt to be fair by the ethnic minorities concerned?
If not, is it possible for these to be changed?

4 Are equal opportunity clauses written into all agreements with trade unions or staff associations?
Would it be helpful to discuss measures to eliminate discrimination and disadvantage regularly with all worker representatives?

5 Do the unions or staff associations appear to be effective channels of communication for the ethnic minority groups in the organization?
Are there any indications that members of ethnic minorities are using, or will be using, alternative channels?
What should the organization's policy be if this occurs?

Affirmative action

We have already presented the case in favour of action to eliminate racial discrimination and disadvantage. In some situations, curtailing obvious discrimination will not be sufficient and workers from ethnic minority groups might still be unable to surmount the artificial barriers which limit their involvement and effectiveness in the organization. Positive action will be needed to encourage and assist these workers so that they might make contributions commensurate with their real potential. This was the rationale behind the affirmative action exception in the 1976 Act. The nature of such a programme of affirmative action will depend on the specific needs of the organization. For example, it may be necessary and feasible for an affirmative action programme to be introduced on a wide front. In some situations it may be advisable initially to tackle particular issues in limited functions or levels of the organization. Each organization will need to design its own programme. A few suggestions for affirmative action based on the practical experience of others are included here. In order to be consistent, they are listed under the headings of recruitment and selection, promotion and transfer, induction and training, and industrial relations.

It is of the utmost importance to remember in viewing these programmes that in no way is it being suggested that anyone should be given preference because of his racial origin or skin colour. The Race Relations Act 1976 proscribes unfair discrimination on the grounds of ethnicity irrespective of who is victim and who is persecutor. The programmes are meant to remove disadvantage, not to give advantage. If this is made clear and employee representatives are involved in devising, or have given their agreement to, the programme it is far less likely to generate resentment in the rest of the workforce.

Recruitment and selection

If an organization suspects that appropriately able members of the ethnic minorities in the local working population are not applying for jobs with the organization, a number of actions can be taken to correct this. Advertisements may be placed in the minority press or other suitably orientated media. Public and private agencies can be informed of the organization's needs. Any existing employees belonging to minority groups provide an effective means of communicating with suitable applicants. Attempts can be made to forge links with local community and race relations agencies. These and similar strategies should mean that the organization improves its communication with potential employees amongst the local ethnic minority community.

If the organization has certain non job-related selection criteria that are discouraging black applicants, these may be waived or amended (not just for black applicants but completely). Perhaps the most controversial issue concerns language requirements. It is undeniable that the ability to speak good English is often essential and always desirable. But in some jobs immigrants with fairly poor English have proved to be excellent members of organizations. Many organizations have been pleased to employ such workers when labour shortages existed. If language proficiency is the only barrier which prevents these workers becoming effective members of the organization at present, then language training provides a good solution in most cases.

Whilst it is possible that tests may be an aid to objective selection generally, they can unfairly discriminate against certain minority groups:

A test is suspect when:
(a) It is given in a language in which a significant number of minority group applicants are not proficient and where language proficiency is not a requirement of the job
(b) It is used in the transfer and promotion of minority group employees to positions which they would already be occupying but for past discriminatory practices.[41]

In addition, tests, the products of Western cultures, can often discriminate against people from other cultures . . . and the same tests are not necessarily reliable for different ethnic groups.[42]

Hence testing should be discontinued unless the organization has evidence of a particular test's validity with regard to ethnic minorities (that is, unless it has 'empirical data demonstrating that the test is predictive of or significantly correlated with important elements of work behaviour relevant to the job for which the candidate is being evaluated.'[43]

Promotion and transfer

The largest organization included in our study was so convinced of the arguments in favour of affirmative action on the matter of promotion to the supervisor level that it had developed medium range targets or quotas for numbers of black supervisors. Although the Race Relations Act 1976 brought an end to this plan, the company still believes it to be in its own interests to remove the barriers which prevent black supervisors emerging from shopfloor situations where virtually everyone is black. This can be done by providing special training or preparation for black applicants which is allowable under the 1976 Act. If any workers of other races demand the same treatment, this should of course be made available to them. Often in an organization the factors restricting promotion opportunities for members of ethnic minorities are specific to that organization, consequently an investigation to identify these factors will probably be needed. On the basis of this information, the organization can then devise a suitable strategy to remove any disadvantage due to race.

Once again, it should be remembered that although special help and assistance may be given to unfairly disadvantaged groups, the eventual selection must be on the ground of merit alone.

Any existing promotion policies or procedures involving age or experience requirements may in fact discriminate against immigrants. If the validity of such requirements is in any way suspect, they should no longer be applied.

Induction and training

A suitably modified induction programme can pay especially large dividends in ethnic minorities. An induction programme is not likely to be really effective if it is confined to the usual first half or one day 'let's show you where everything is' event. If after evaluating previous experience a specially adapted programme can be devised for specific ethnic groups, this may mean that an excellent start is made to reducing disadvantage.

Workers from different cultures or subcultures can be properly introduced to the organization's practices, values and culture. With immigrants from cultures very different from our own, this may mean discussions on such elementary considerations as what is a manager?, what is hard work?, merit? potential?

An organization can also take affirmative action to encourage members of ethnic minority groups to take up opportunities for skills training. What may be done is illustrated by the way in which one company assisted black youths to enter a craft apprenticeship scheme. The company, which had a large contingent of black workers in its workforce, was concerned that too few black youths were entering the scheme. This was attributed to the academic qualifications normally required for entry into apprenticeship. It was decided that an alternative means of entry should be tried. With the agreement of all concerned, the company selected a number of youths using criteria such as manual dexterity and willingness to learn. The successful interviewees were then admitted to a 'pre-apprenticeship course'. This course involved block-release to a local technical college and the trainees received both on- and off-the-job instruction. At the end of the course, all the black youths were admitted to the apprenticeship scheme proper, where they were said to be performing admirably.

An effective means of getting more ethnic minority workers to take up skills training is by individual counselling. The training needs of each employee can be continually assessed and details of appropriate opportunities for development may then be brought to his or her attention.

Although a number of managers we consulted saw no reason to provide language training for employees, in several cases it was clear that the opportunities for development for many black workers were severely constrained by their poor proficiency in English. We have already given an example of a language training course providing both commercial benefit for the company and improved prospects for workers. There is little doubt that such courses can be highly beneficial and in some instances they are vital. However, we believe that they will have little chance of success unless they are accompanied by actions of other kinds. If people see no reason to take part in language training, they are unlikely to make full use of this opportunity. Language training will be relevant to workers if it is related to jobs and working environment but it will be even more meaningful to them if it is accompanied by other forms of affirmative action.

Industrial relations

The greatest catalyst for racial conflict is ignorance. Better race relations may therefore be encouraged by the considered and well-managed provision of relevant information. This might mean giving details of the background of Asians (see Appendix Two) to managers and supervisors so that they are better able to understand the behaviour of these members of the workforce. Contesting some of the racial myths about black people in our society with facts might be useful on a much wider front and the information provided at the beginning of Part I may prove useful in this context.

On the basis of our investigations we would suggest that considerable benefit could accrue to organizations that can increase the awareness of their managers about racial discrimination and its outcomes. As we reported earlier all too often managers appear to turn a blind eye (consciously or otherwise) to racial discrimination and disadvantage. Disregarding crude prejudice we believe that this 'lack of awareness' is due to several factors. Most organizations do not have substantial proportions of black workers so the characteristics of management of a multi-racial workforce are not commonly shared, and are not given (or paid) much attention in management journals or other forums for discussion. The severity of the country's economic problems and the need to focus attention elsewhere have meant further neglect of this issue. Another factor is the reticence of the ethnic minorities themselves to protest against discrimination and disadvantage. This might be disputed by some managers who claim that many black workers have chips on their shoulders. But there is little doubt that as yet ethnic minorities have not cooperated to pursue their own interests nearly as effectively as they might.

Those managers who consciously disregard racial discrimination and disadvantage may opt for inactivity out of fear of causing greater unrest through intervention. This point was made on many occasions during our study and is well exemplified by the statement of one manager whose organization took action only after an investigation by the Race Relations Board: 'The investigation brought it home to us. Without it I do not think we would have paid so much attention to the subject—partly through fear of aggravating matters.'[44]

In the event this organization developed an equal opportunity policy with all levels of the organization contributing to its creation. The exercise was adjudged a success: 'The open nature of the discussions helped to dispel people's fears and the policy is now part of company routine. It's paying off in terms of better use of the workforce and greater understanding between workers.'[45]

All the factors which were contributing to tolerance of racial discrimination and disadvantage add up to poor management. Throughout our study there was a high correlation between the extent of the effort to remove discrimination and disadvantage and the level of development of managerial practice. This was, of course, not at all surprising as race relations is merely one aspect of 'industrial relations'. Organizations which exhibit a constructive approach to this one are therefore more likely to manifest satisfactoriness in the other. The obvious implication is that the elimination of racial discrimination and disadvantage in employment is linked to management development. Affirmative action in this field would certainly increase the rate at which racial harmony in employment becomes a reality.

Good supervision is essential in getting the best out of a workforce, the better supervisors use their extensive knowledge of individuals to encourage them in their work. When a supervisor is ignorant of the strengths, weaknesses and general behaviour of an individual or large group of individuals, this can limit his effectiveness considerably. Consequently, it can pay dividends in terms of productivity and work relations if courses on ethnic minorities are run for supervisors. The content of these courses might include details of background, culture, naming systems, religion, and the communication problems associated with a particular racial group as well as an explanation of the requirements of the Race Relations Act. (Several of the advisory agencies named in Appendix Three can provide details of packaged courses for supervisors.) As well as providing information to members of the workforce, management can also seek every opportunity to build links between otherwise virtually segregated racial groups. One interesting idea that has already been tried with some success is the institution of multi-racial discussion groups. These groups need not confine their subject matter to questions of race. They can discuss all aspects of the organization and its role in the community. Group leaders from outside the organization can be used if necessary. These might come from agencies like the Workers' Educational Association or from ethnic minority associations. As we have already said, building a relationship with such associations can be beneficial to the organization.

It is probable that in most circumstances exercises involving the workforce will have a greater chance of success if they are implemented in association with the union. It is certainly desirable to have union agreement to a company policy on equal opportunity. Additionally, it helps to have race relations clauses written into management-union agreements whenever appropriate. There are advantages to both management and unions in doing this. Management can ensure that policies which are in the interests of production and good industrial relations are more likely to be accepted by all employees. Trade unions can demonstrate to minority groups that they act in the interests of these groups, thus decreasing the possibility that black workers will lose confidence in the existing unions and so form their own negotiating groups.

Monitoring and record keeping

A boardroom edict that the organization will pursue a policy of equal opportunity may be of some merit in itself but real progress depends on that policy being sincerely implemented throughout all aspects of organizational life. The only way to assess the extent to which equality of opportunity is a reality is by systematically collecting data. If it is to monitor and evaluate a policy of non-discrimination or a programme of affirmative action, the organization must have some means of identifying members of ethnic minorities. Some people are strongly opposed to organizations keeping records which indicate an employee's race or colour. Many managers believe that such records are discriminatory in themselves and are unacceptable on principle. Some members of ethnic minorities fear such records, believing that they will be used against them. Others argue against recording race, claiming that it is unnecessary, expensive, impracticable or offensive. We believe that keeping records of ethnic origin or colour can mean that racial discrimination and disadvantage are more speedily eliminated from employing organizations. Bearing the value of this in mind, the various arguments against such records seem less significant. For example, the contention that recording an employee's race is discriminatory in itself is accurate but the same is true for collecting details of sex, age, skill or education. An organization needs this kind of data so that it can be 'discriminating' in its employment of people, placing them in appropriate jobs and giving them suitable opportunities. In other words, this information is essential for efficient management of the enterprise and, if racial discrimination and disadvantage are lowering effectiveness, the organization must have the necessary data to correct this. Seen in this context, such record keeping is justifiable.

The anxiety of members of ethnic minorities about records is understandable. It was clearly an emotive issue for some of the black people we consulted. They felt that such records could be abused and might be the basis for a more systematic approach to racial discrimination (or even oppression). Whilst still being aware of the possibilities of misuse, other black employees we consulted felt that records of race or colour should be supported. One man said 'Without records we are just too bloody many'. It was also pointed out that for many ethnic minorities 'visual inspection' was sufficient for purposes of identification. Recording ethnicity would add little or nothing to their chances of suffering from unfair discrimination. (This fact was brought home to us forcefully when we discovered that the personnel files of black employees in one organization which claimed not to keep records of racial origin were nevertheless informally marked.)

The possibility that requesting and recording the ethnic origin of employees may prove offensive makes it essential that members of the workforce should be fully consulted. Management should make quite clear what the interest is in keeping such records and it might also indicate the ways in which this monitoring could be done. The two basic approaches are either to undertake periodic censuses or to keep details of ethnic origin in the permanent personnel records system. Each of these may have attractions in given circumstances and a combination of both may be desirable. The census approach has the major limitation of providing just a snapshot impression; if only one of these approaches is to be used, keeping a permanent record is likely to be much more revealing and more convenient. A decision to start keeping records of race will probably mean that an initial census is essential.

Methods of monitoring

Four bases for classification may be identified:[46]

1 *Nationality* Many firms record the nationality of job applicants and employees. For the purpose of monitoring an equal opportunity policy, this information is not a useful variable, since many coloured people in this country are British citizens and this will increasingly be true. Nationality does not therefore provide a good guide to race, colour or ethnic origins.

2 *Place of birth* This information too is commonly recorded. But like nationality it does not provide a good basis for monitoring an equal opportunity policy, since increasing numbers of black people will have been born in this country and the information will not provide a sound indicator of race, colour or ethnic origins.

3 *Colour* Classification of individuals as coloured or white would provide some useful information but it would not allow comparison of different groups of black workers. A more refined analysis could be based on a classification such as black, brown and white, whereby people of West Indian and African origins or descent would be classified as black, people of Asian origins as brown and those of European origins as white. Such a

classification would inevitably require subjective judgement in many cases.

4 *Ethnic origins* On this basis, people might simply be classified as being of African, Asian, European or West Indian origin or descent. This would provide a classification very similar to that by colour described above. It would also allow other classifications to be included, for example, North African, Chinese, Cypriot and so on, as and if required by particular circumstances.

On the basis of its experience the old Race Relations Board concluded that classification by ethnic origin is probably the most suitable for purposes of monitoring. It was claimed that using ethnic origin 'avoids the problems of nationality and place of birth, in that it provides a close proxy for race and colour, and is a flexible system which can be readily adapted and expanded to suit particular circumstances. It also avoids the problem of defining "colour" '.[47] Whilst the experience of our study suggests that in many instances ethnic origin will be a highly suitable classification we did find examples of organizations successfully using alternative systems. This serves as a further illustration that the one best way approach is inappropriate. What may be cost effective and feasible for one organization may be too expensive and impracticable for another. Each organization will have to decide what method or combination of methods best suits its needs.

Collecting information

Whatever method of recording or system of classification is decided upon, the organization will need to have some means of allocating each employee to a particular category. Basically there are two ways of doing this: an observer can record the data or the employee may be asked to identify himself with a particular category.

Using an observer can be problematical because of the subjectivity of the judgements made. With this method of recording it is therefore essential that comprehensive guidelines and some training be given to observers. This will help to improve consistency but accuracy will always be limited to some degree for the obvious reason that some people cannot be readily allocated to any single category. In certain cases the only meaningful way to determine ethnic origin or colour is for the individual concerned to say what he or she thinks or feels on this issue. To do this, means that the major objection to self-classification will need to be faced: the possibility that some people will regard this enquiry as offensive. It is possible that asking just a few individuals to classify themselves whilst most others are allocated to a particular category by an observer will create more hostile reactions than the operation of self-classification for all. Despite these potential difficulties, using an observer can be an effective way to proceed. We found one example of a very large employer using trained interviewers to classify employees according to colour and place of birth. The grid below was used.

	Born in UK	Born outside UK
White		
Non-white		

Although this is a very simple classification it can nevertheless be effective as a means of monitoring non-discrimination or affirmative action programmes. Classification by observers is probably best confined to such simple systems.

Self classification is less likely to give offence if it is implemented after full discussion with all existing members of the organization. Full consultation will help all employees to understand the purposes of asking questions on race and will mean that this practice will become part of the organization's culture. As such, it is unlikely to cause lasting or major offence to new recruits. One means of asking for an applicant's or employee's ethnic origin is by using the following model paragraph and coding on an application form or questionnaire:

> This company operates an equal opportunity policy to ensure that all people receive equal treatment in employment regardless of their race, colour or ethnic or national origins. In order to assist us in checking that this policy is fully carried out, and for no other reason, would you please provide the necessary information by ticking the appropriate box.
> I would describe myself as of
>
> African origins................ ☐
> Asian origins.................. ☐
> European origins............ ☐
> West Indian origins.......... ☐
> Other (please specify)....... ☐ 48

Greater precision can be obtained if some definitions of ethnic origin (as used by the organization) are appended to the application form or questionnaire.

Use of data

When an organization is able to identify employees by ethnic origin or colour appropriate statistical analyses may then be produced. These will provide a factual basis for reviewing equal opportunity in the organization and will help in assessing the need for intervention. It would be naïve to suggest that trust should be placed in numbers alone. Statistics by themselves may not be taken as determinants of 'what needs doing where' as they may sometimes be misleading. For example, very small proportions of minority group workers in skilled grades of employment cannot be said to show conclusively that equality of opportunity for entry to those grades does not exist. Factors other than racial discrimination may be responsible for this phenomenon. Similarly, showing that white and black workers both get promoted to supervisor level in numbers commensurate with their presence in the shop floor workforce is not proof of equal opportunity. It may be that judged according to relevant criteria, there should be more black supervisors than white. Statistics will only provide an objective description of the distribution and movement of minority groups employees throughout the organization. It is the task of management to interpret this data and then decide what action is necessary in order to promote equal opportunity for all members of the organization.

In our study of a sample of organizations only a small minority kept records but several others had conducted periodic surveys. Over half the participating organizations said that they would probably start keeping records as a result of the passing of the 1976 Act. In discussions with managers it appeared that, principally because of a limitation on resources, few would be able to undertake sophisticated analyses of data on ethnic minorities. Most managers felt that it would be most useful (and as much as they could handle) to determine how ethnic groups were distributed throughout the various departments, functions and levels of the organization. This analysis would help to identify significant differences between racial groups which might then be subjected to further investigation.

Several managers said that it would not be difficult for their organization to analyse recruitment, training and promotion practices with a view to assessing equality of opportunity. Keeping details of all applications with reasons for the eventual decision did seem feasible and in addition to discouraging direct discrimination this would highlight any differences in success rates of applicants. The existence of such differences could then be examined and the criteria used in selecting for recruitment, training or promotion could be reviewed for unjustifiable indirect discrimination.

In the few cases we met where organizations had kept records of ethnic origin or colour for some time, it was disappointing to see how little use had been made of this data. The attitude of some managers seemed to be that 'it's there if ever it's wanted'. It is difficult to believe that any organization can be serious about ensuring equal opportunity if it does not use available information to monitor existing practices and policies or to plan for the future. A sincere desire to eliminate racial discrimination will mean that the data on ethnic minorities are regularly analysed and reviewed but it is more important that follow-up action should be taken when a need is indicated.

Conclusion

The nature and mode of presentation of the information we have given were chosen with a view to providing assistance to managers. Members of the management team are by no means the only people who have either a responsibility or a need to tackle racial discrimination. In particular we would suggest that individual members of racial majority groups themselves could do more to aid the development of true equality of opportunity and racial harmony. Nevertheless, as far as most organizations are concerned, it is managers who will have the job of deciding what could and should be done to improve race relations and to ensure equality of opportunity for all. Regrettably, the experience of our study suggests that many managers lack awareness of the impact of racial discrimination and disadvantage on their organizations. We have already offered a variety of possible explanations for this as, on the basis of our study, we do not believe that prejudice is the sole cause of this lack of awareness.

Organizations which tolerate racial discrimination and disadvantage are likely to face even greater penalties in the future. Consequently the role of the manager in this respect will become even more demanding. Race relations in employment is just one aspect of industrial relations and the quality of relationships between races in an organization is a significant determinant of organizational climate. Also, as we believe that the effects of racial discrimination extend beyond its immediate victims, such unfair treatment can create or exacerbate negative attitudes and so limit productivity. Seen in this context the elimination of discrimination and the promotion of racial harmony are not only essential to social justice, they are also vital to economic performance.

APPENDIX 1

Some further statistics on racial minorities

Table 1 Numbers of people living in Great Britain who were born overseas

In 1971, just under 3 million people (2,983,140) living in Great Britain were born overseas, forming 5.5 per cent of the total population of nearly 54 million. The following table gives the countries from which the largest numbers came:

Country of birth	*Number resident in Great Britain*
Ireland	709,235
Africa	164,205
India	321,995
West Indies*	304,070
Germany	157,680
Pakistan'	139,935
America	131,540
Poland	110,925
Cyprus	73,295

* And other countries specified under America

'The number for Pakistan includes people from Bangladesh.

(Source Census 1971, Great Britain, Country of Birth Tables)

These figures do not include the children born in this country to people born overseas (Table 2). But they do include a number of British people born abroad (for example, children of diplomatic and army staffs) who should not be included as members of particular ethnic minorities. This applies particularly to the figures given for those born in India and Pakistan. It should be noted that the figures for Africa include East African Asians.

Table 2 Major ethnic groups in black population (in thousands)

Area of parental origin	*Place of birth*			*UK born as percentage of total*
	Area of origin	*UK*	*Total*	
Africa	119.5	48.5	168.0	29
West Indies	222.9	223.3	446.2	50
India	256.3	226.8	483.1	47
Pakistan	128.3	41.4	169.7	24
Total	727.0	540.0	1,267.0	43

(Source Census 1971, The Coloured Population of Great Britain, by GB Gillian Lomas)

Table 3 Geographical distribution of black population

The following table shows how each of the four main racial groups listed in Table 2 was distributed in 1971:

Distribution by region for selected birthplace groups, England and Wales, 1971

	United Kingdom	*Africa*	*West Indies*	*India*	*Pakistan*	*Africa, W Indies India an Pakistan*
Total number	45,585,200 = 100%	134,350 = 100%	299,580 = 100%	274,545 = 100%	131,885 = 100%	840,33 = 100%
Region:						
North York	7.1	0.6	0.3	0.8	2.0	0.8
& Humberside	10.1	2.8	5.0	5.9	19.7	7.3
North West	14.2	5.9	4.6	6.6	14.9	7.0
E Midlands	7.1	7.1	4.9	7.4	3.5	5.8
W Midlands	10.5	7.6	15.2	20.9	20.9	16.7
E Anglia	3.5	1.3	1.1	1.0	1.2	1.1
S East	33.8	70.4	65.3	53.8	35.6	57.7
S West	7.9	3.7	3.0	3.3	1.4	3.0
Wales	5.8	0.6	0.6	0.4	1.1	0.6

(Source The Census 1971, The Coloured Population of Great Britain, G B Gillian Lomas. Figures used in this table are based on the 100 per ce data from the 1971 Census and do not agree exactly with those used in Table which are based on the 1 per cent data. The figures in this table are more like to be accurate.)

Table 4 Distribution of black working population by industry
The following table gives the types of industry in which most coloured people work, compared with the general population

	West Indian %	*Pakistani/ Bangladeshi* %	*Indian* %	*African/ Asian* %	*General population* %
Shipbuilding and vehicles	7	12	12	6	4
Textiles	1	26	10	6	2
Construction	7	1	4	7	7
Transport and communication	10	5	12	11	7
Distributive trades	3	7	9	15	13
Professional and scientific services	19	2	6	3	12

(Source The Facts of Racial Disadvantage, by D J Smith, PEP, 1976)

This table indicates the large numbers of Indians and Pakistanis in vehicle manufacture and of Pakistanis in the textile industry. Of those in the distributive trades, 38 per cent were self-employed as shopkeepers and many of those categorized as employees were probably working in family shops. The high proportion of West Indians in the professional and scientific services was partly due to the large number of West Indian women working as nurses and secretaries.

These tables are based on information given in a briefing paper prepared by Claire Demuth, Runnymede Trust, for the Community Relations Commission's Trade Union Consultative Committee.

APPENDIX 2

The background of Asian minority groups

Generalizations about the cultural, social and religious backgrounds of ethnic minority groups can be very misleading, just as generalizations about the English or Europeans can be.

Asian cultures contain a wide range of different customs and beliefs and, as in most countries, people can vary considerably in their personal convictions and life styles.

The following background information is therefore intended as general guidance rather than for strict interpretation. The emphasis has been placed on describing Asian cultural backgrounds, as these are often seen as the most different from the Western way of life. The way in which the different cultures affect Asians living and working in the UK is more difficult to summarize, but detailed guidance on this can be obtained from the organizations and publications set out in Appendix 3.

The family

The Asian family is, in general, a joint or extended family, consisting of mother, father, sons and sons' families. Daughters leave home on marriage to live in the home of the husband. The joint family traditionally live together and decisions are taken by the head of the family in consultation with all the members.

One important difference between this system and European traditions is the role of the individual family member, for whom family responsibilities and duties are more important than individual wishes. This can sometimes produce a different outlook from that of a society which emphasizes individual development, such as that in Britain. Asian families living in the UK are more likely to be split up and the joint family may not always be so wide.

Religion

Asian religions are Hinduism, Islam, Sikhism, Jainism, Buddhism, Christianity and others.

Pakistan is an Islamic State, which means that nearly all Pakistanis are Muslims. India and Bangladesh are not single religious states: India has a main population of Hindus but there are also large numbers of Muslims and Sikhs, as well as many Christians, Jains, Parsees and other groups. Most Bangladeshis in the UK are Muslims.

Marriage

The majority of Asian marriages are arranged. Marriage is regarded as being a linking of families rather than individuals and the bride joins the husband's family after marriage. The system of arranged marriage is often difficult to understand for a Western society which emphasizes the freedom of individuals to choose their marriage partners, and where the circles in which young people find their partners may be removed from those of their parents. The arranged marriage, however, takes place in the context of a society which emphasizes religious duty and family life, and where social activities outside the family circle may not be very wide for young people. Parents choose partners for their children from families which are known to them and which are approved of by them, and use this knowledge to assess compatibility. In the atmosphere of the UK, a number of Asian minorities are gradually adapting to marriage of choice, independent of caste or family restrictions.

Names

Names and wrongly naming can be a sensitive area for everyone and when both the names and the naming systems are unfamiliar, mistakes can easily happen.

Muslims, Sikhs and Hindus have different naming systems. There are also regional differences and names which denote caste or sub-caste.

Sikh names always include Singh as the middle name for a man and Kaur for a woman. Amongst Hindus, the suffix 'bhai,' meaning brother ('ben' for sister), is often added to a name amongst close friends, or 'ji' is added as a term of respect. 'Swami' (for Hindus), or 'Imam' or Ulmas (for Muslims), means a religious teacher and is used generally in the same sense as Reverend in the West. One of the most familiar Gujarati names is 'Patel', which has similar popularity to 'Smith' in the UK. Muslim names include one name, such as

Muhammad, Ahmad, Syed, Rasul etc, for a man, and Fatima, Amina, Qawar (Un-Nisa), for a woman. These religious names could be before or after the other names, like *Muhammad* Akhtar, or Salim *Ahmad*. For women, Bibi or Begum is usually at the end of the name to denote female status. But it should be noted there are no hard and fast rules about Muslim names.

Basically, the best way to find out how a person should be addressed is to ask him or her, and to discuss with them how their naming system could be brought into the British system. Unacceptable nicknames or short cuts, such as Singh 3, can cause resentment and should be avoided. More detailed advice on names can be obtained from the National Centre for Industrial Language Training or from the CRE.

Language

Asian languages vary considerably. In the Asian sub-continent there are about 20 major languages (and many more dialects) with as much in common as, say, Russian and English. This means that in many cases Asians from different regions of the same country cannot understand each other's language.

Languages used by the main groups which have settled in the UK include Urdu, Gujarati, Punjabi, Hindi, Bengali. Others include Tamil and Malayalam.

East African Asians

East African Asians are often looked upon as a different group from others, and to some extent their pattern of migration to this country via East Africa (often as forced migrants) may have made them so. English language ability may be higher and they may be considered more Westernized than other Asians in some cases, but East African Asians still identify strongly with their Asian religions and cultural backgrounds.

Asian religious groups

Hindus

Hinduism is often defined as a way of life rather than a religion, covering a vast range of human activity outside the scope of religion.

For the orthodox Hindu, worship (Puja) is centred on the home, and religious and ceremonial rites are performed by the eldest member when all the members of the family gather together. Temple worship is also important on special occasions and in the UK Hindu Temples are beginning to be established.

Hindus worship many gods but ultimately One God, as they believe that both gods and men emanate from one eternal creative force. The religious aim of life is to be drawn back to the divine origin and to be released from the need to be reborn. Reincarnation is therefore of central importance, and behaviour in this life determines status in the next life. Various different Hindu sects differ in their interpretation of ultimate salvation, some believing in reabsorption in divinity, others maintaining a distinction between God and individual souls, similar to Christianity.

The caste system determines social position. Traditionally, there were four main castes: 1) Brahmin, priestly caste; 2) Kshatriya, the warrier and ruling caste; 3) Vaishya, the caste of farmers, merchants and craftsmen; 4) Shudra, the caste of servants. There are also many sub-castes. Each caste was exclusive of the other and intermarriage disapproved of. In modern times the strict caste system has been gradually liberalised and it is now forbidden by law in India to discriminate on grounds of caste.

Indian society has changed radically since ancient times when the caste system had an important social function, and today it lingers largely as a traditional code without the strict relationship to society as a whole. There is a considerable amount of misunderstanding in the UK about the caste system and its application here.

The Hindu calendar has a large number of festivals, some of which are centred on the seasons of the year; others are connected with the legendary history of gods and goddesses. Three of the most important are Diwali, Holi and Navratri (leading up to Dashera). Diwali is a festival of lights observed in October-November, marking the start of the Hindu New Year. Holi is a festival of colours observed at the start of spring. Navratri/Dashera is an autumn festival including 10 day celebrations, with folk dancing, devotional songs and music and religious processions.

Hindu marriages are important social occasions, often involving a family in great expense. The ceremonies, which are highly symbolic, are crowned by a feast to which as many people as possible are invited, after which the newly-weds as a rule go to live with the family of the bridegroom. In the majority of cases the marriage itself will have been arranged by the relatives of the couple, full account having been taken of caste, sub-caste, kinship and horoscope. Horoscopes are part of a traditional pattern of Hindu religious life, involving the choosing of auspicious days for important ceremonies.

As in any other religion, not all followers of the Hindu religion observe all the prescribed practices. There are, however, certain social customs and modes of behaviour which need to be understood and respected. Principal among these are an emphasis on personal hygiene and methods of cooking and eating food. In Hindu religious philosophy, the eating of meat is strongly forbidden, particularly beef, since the cow is a sacred animal. Most Hindus will not eat fish, eggs or foods containing eggs and as diet has a strong religious aspect, it is important to ascertain such matters when dealing with Hindus in order to avoid giving offence. Although many Hindus are strictly vegetarian, a few have adapted themselves to Western customs of meat eating. The drinking of alcohol and smoking of tobacco are religiously and socially disapproved of and therefore far less common than in Western countries.

Muslims

A person who believes in Islam is a Muslim. To a Muslim, Islam is a way of life, governing not only religious practice and morality but social relationships, marriage, divorce, kinship, economic and political relations among Muslims. There are five pillars of Islam: first, the declaration of faith—there is no deity except Allah (God) and Muhammad is His last prophet and messenger; second, five daily prayers at appointed times; third, *Zakat*, compulsory alms-giving to the poor (2½% per annum) of a man's accumulated wealth; fourth, fasting during the month of Ramadan, and fifth,. making the pilgrimage to Mecca. The Muslims believe that the Holy Qur'an is the true, revealed word of Allah and His final revelations for the guidance of mankind.

The Muslim family is usually an extended family with different relations having different responsibilities. Islam affirms the equality of men and women as human beings, but rules for the sexes are different and free mixing between the two is disapproved of. Traditionally, women should cover their heads and bodies and avoid contact with unrelated men. Broadly speaking, this practice is called 'purdah', or veiling. Islam enjoins marriage.

Islam has been codified into five categories of practical rules: obligatory duties; recommended but not obligatory; indifferent; disapproved of; and forbidden areas to which punishments are attached. The major offences include adultery, fornication, drinking of spirits, using intoxicants, disobeying parents, eating meat from pigs or animals that have died naturally, delaying the time of prayers without proper excuse, not observing the fast in Ramadan, eating non-halal meat and taking interest from others for self-gain.

There are five daily prayers, before which hands and feet must be washed. The mouth and nose should be rinsed and wet hands should be passed over the head. Midday prayers on Friday must be said in a group; other prayers can be said individually. During the month of Ramadan fasting takes place from dawn to dusk. There are two important Islamic festivals: *Eid-ul-Fitre*, celebrated at the end of the fasting month of Ramadan, and *Eid-ul-Adha*, celebrated on the 10th of the Islamic calendar month of Dhul-Haji to commemorate the sacrifice of Prophet Ishmael by the Prophet Abraham.

Misconceptions are common in the UK about polygamy among Muslims. In practice, Muslims in this country have one wife only; and in Pakistan, although it is possible to have more than one wife, the permission of first wife and court permission is essential. Most Muslims in Britain are from Pakistan and Bangladesh.

Religious observance varies according to the individual's circumstances and facilities available.

Sikhs

The Sikh religion is the youngest of the major world religions, being about 500 years old. Its founder, Guru Nanak, was born in 1469 in a village near Lahore in the Punjab (North West India), which now forms part of Pakistan. He was followed by nine successors, all called Gurus; the last of these died in 1708. Sikhism was therefore developed by a continuous evolutionary process over about 200 years—a process which is unique in the history of world religions.

Although there are apparent resemblances with the other two religions in India at the time of its founding (Hinduism and Islam), the originality and distinct features of the Sikh religion make it a 'new and direct revelation'.

There are two categories of Sikhs: Saihajdharis and Amritdharis; the former are termed 'apprentices' and are not required to be very orthodox in their approach. They may or may not keep long hair or wear the other symbols described below. The latter are those who have been formally baptised and must therefore keep rigidly to the disciplines and code of conduct enjoined upon them at the time of baptism. These Sikhs are called the Khalsa (the pure ones) and do keep the following five Ks:

1) Keshas—long hair
2) Kangha—comb
3) Kara—steel bracelet
4) Kirpan—a small sword or dagger
5) Kachha—a special undergarment like shorts.

As the long hair must be properly tied up into a knot at the top of the head, the turban has inevitably become a religious necessity and symbol.

Sikhism accepts the equality and brotherhood of man, and gives women equal status and rights with men. The caste system does not exist in the Sikh religion. All Sikhs therefore take the surname 'Singh' which means lion, and women's names end with 'Kaur'.

Marriage is seen as the bringing together of two families, as well as the close relationship of man and woman. The system of arranged marriages has decreased in modern, educated society and it is also now decreasing in rural areas. The society is evolving a new system in which the boy and girl have a definite say in the choice of partner and are allowed to meet each other before mariage.

There are no hard and fast rules of diet and dress, but smoking is strictly prohibited. The Sikh Gurus have laid down general rules of conduct on food and dress but these are open to interpretation according to personal inclinations. Some Sikhs (but very few) would include meat eating in the category of food to be avoided but most do eat meat, although not from animals slaughtered in the semitic method (Halal or Kosher). The Sikh scriptures do not restrict the eating of beef but because of the Hindu influence a large number of Sikhs do not eat beef. All intoxicants, including alcohol, should as far as possible be avoided.

More detailed information on the background of Asian minority groups may be found in the following publications:

The Background & Employment of Asian Immigrants, T C Jupp and Evelyn Davies, Runnymede Trust

East Comes West—A Background to Some Asian Faiths, Community Relations Commission

The Indian Family in Britain, Dilip Hiro, Community Relations Commission

Between Two Cultures—A Study in Relationships between Generations in the Asian Community in Britain, Community Relations Commission

A Guide to Asian Names, Community Relations Commission

Calendar of Religious Festivals, Community Relations Commission

This Appendix was prepared by the Community Relations Commission

APPENDIX 3

Some notes on relevant agencies and advisory bodies

The following are some of the agencies which managers may wish to contact for information or other assistance.

Commission for Racial Equality
Address Elliot House
Allington Street
London SW1
Telephone 01-828-7022

The Commission for Racial Equality (CRE) is the successor to the Race Relations Board and Community Relations Commission.

The CRE has the following duties:

a) to work toward the elimination of discrimination
b) to promote equality of opportunity, and good relations, between persons of different racial groups generally; and
c) to keep under review the working of the Act, and when they are so required by the Secretary of State or otherwise thought to be necessary, to draw up and submit to the Secretary of State proposals for amending it.

The CRE has the power to conduct formal investigations for any purpose connected with the carrying out of its duties, and may carry out research and educational activities. It may also choose to provide advice and assistance to individual complainants taking their cases before a court or industrial tribunal.

Local Community Relations Councils
There are 91 community relations councils (CRCs) throughout the country and these vary in size and in the methods by which they are

funded. The majority of CRCs were constituted in conjunction with the Community Relations Commission, but a number of them are local bodies of a similar nature in areas without a CRC, or subcommittees of the local authority or Council of Social Service.

All CRCs have constitutions which provide for local organizations to be affiliated to them, as well as having a proportion of individual members.

Most councils elect an executive committee and appoint a number of specialist sub-committees concerned with topics such as housing, employment and education and with powers to co-opt interested individuals.

Their regional distribution is as follows:

Greater London	28	East Midlands	8
South West England	9	North West England	12
South East England	11	North East England	10
West Midlands	9	Scotland	3
Wales	1		

A full list of CRCs, showing their addresses and officers is available from the Commission for Racial Equality.

Department of Employment Race Relations Advisers

There are 18 Race Relations Employment Advisers (RREAs), four of whom are part-time. They work closely with the agencies of the Manpower Services Commission and provide a specialist service to help both sides of industry to handle questions that may arise in a multi-racial workforce. Inquiries about work permits may be channelled through the Advisers.

RREAs are located in the Department of Employment's regions, and their addresses are as follows:

South East Region
Fourth Floor
Lonsdale Chambers
27 Chancery Lane
London WC2
01-405-8454

East Midlands Region
Commercial House
Thurland Street
Nottingham NG1 3DE
0602-411-081

Midlands Region
2 Duchess Place
Hagley Road
Birmingham B16 8NS
021-455-7111

North West Region
Sunley Building
Piccadilly Plaza
Manchester M60 7JS
061-832-9111

Northern Region
Wellbar House
Gallowgate
Newcastle-upon-Tyne
0632-27575

South West Region
The Pithay
Bristol BS1 2NQ
0272-291071

Yorkshire & Humberside
City House
Leeds LS1 4JH
0532-38232

Wales
Branch B2, 4th Floor
Companies House
Crown Way
Maindy, Cardiff CF4 3VW
0222-388-588

Scotland
43 Jeffrey Street
Edinburgh EH3 8YX
031-556-8433

The London Graduate School of Business Studies: The minority group's case study project

Address John Brock, Project Manager
London Graduate School of Business Studies
Sussex Place
Regent's Park
London NW1 4SA
Telephone 01-723-9024

The Case Study Project at the London Business School is a major exercise aimed at distilling experience of the issues and problems raised by the employment of minority groups and making it available to trade unionists and managers for education and training purposes. Case studies involving some 60 to 70 organizations are being prepared. These will be available both as individual cases and in book form. Groups of case writers have been based at the following:

> The London Business School, Loughborough University, Aston Management Centre, Bradford Management Centre, Lancaster University, University of Manchester Institute of Science & Technology and Thames Polytechnic.

The National Centre for Industrial Language Training (NCILT)

Address Tom Jupp
National Centre for Industrial Language Training
Pathway Centre, Recreation Road
Southall, Middlesex UB2 5PF
Telephone 01-571-3115

Local specialist units in 26 centres throughout the country provide training in communications within a multi-racial workforce (addresses and telephone numbers for the local centres may be obtained from the above address). The service includes identifying specific training needs and developing purpose-built training courses.

In-company training for personnel, training and first-line managers and for shop stewards covers:

—information on the background and employment of workers from overseas
—exercises on overcoming communication breakdowns
—opportunities to participate in the language training programme for non-English speaking workers
—seminars and working groups to consider current practices and policies in the workplace

Language training programmes for workers from overseas include:

—basic, intensive courses in elementary spoken English
—more advanced courses with special emphasis on particular needs, eg language for safety training, operator training, etc
—communications courses for supervisors, line minders, instructors, etc.

The units serviced by the Government funded National Centre for Industrial Language Training form a nationally coordinated scheme for training in the multi-racial workforce. NCILT offers an information service, a staff training programme and has a resources centre with printed and audio visual materials.

The Runnymede Trust
Address Dr M A Pearn
62 Chandos Place
London WC2
Telephone 01-836-3266

The Runnymede Trust is a registered educational charity which was established in 1968. The main objectives of the Trust are the collection and dissemination of information, and the promotion of public education on immigration and race relations. The objectives of the Trust are carried out by a number of means:

An information service which provides accurate and up to date information on race relations and immigration
A monthly information bulletin

Publications, including pamphlets, occasional studies and briefing papers, on matters of current concern
Seminars and meetings
Specialist education work in industry
A major census analysis project.

The main work of the Trust in the employment field is the Race Relations Training Project which aims to encourage the development of training in this area for supervisors and managers, as well as the preparation of training materials for use by others. The project is financed by the Training Services Agency and is directed by Dr M A Pearn. The trust is also in a position to give advice and help on the use of selection tests with ethnic minority workers.

Minority organizations and associations

The following is a list of the names and addresses of contacts for a few of the larger minority organizations and associations. It should be noted that this is by no means a full selection and the *Directory of Ethnic Minority Organizations* (CRC) may be consulted for a comprehensive list.

West Indian Standing Conference
G Ince
46 Lydford Road
London W9 3LX

Standing Conference of Asian Organizations in the UK
Chairman
Dr A F A Sayeed
2 Mickleton Drive
Leicester LE5 6GD

Standing Conference of African Organizations in the UK
U A Ejionye
119 Norfold Avenue
Palmers Green
London N13 6AL

Confederation of Indian Organizations (UK)
K Nagda
11 North Avenue
Harrow
Middlesex HA2 7AE

Standing Conference of Pakistani Organizations in the UK
President
Councillor B Mann JP
City Chambers
Glasgow G2 1DU

Indian Workers Association
President
A S Rai
18 Featherstone Road
Southall
Middlesex

Federation of Bangladesh Associations
National Governor
S A Rasul
2 Marchwood Road
Sheffield 6

APPENDIX 4

Race and employment: a short reading list

1 BOSENQUET N, *Race and Employment in Britain,* Runnymede Trust, 1973
2 BROOKS D, *Black Employment in the Black Country: A Study of Walsall,* Runnymede Trust, 1975
3 CAMPBELL-PLATT K, *Ethnic Minorities in Society: A reference guide,* Cambridge University Press, 1970
4 CBI, *Race Relations in Employment,* Confederation of British Industry, 1970
5 CRC, *Ethnic Minorities in Britain—Statistical Data, 1976, Some of My Best Friends. A Report on Race Relations Attitudes,* 1976
6 DANIEL W W, *Racial Discrimination in England,* Penguin, 1968
7 DEPARTMENT of EMPLOYMENT, *Take Seven. A Study of Race Relations in Seven Companies,* HMSO, 1972
8 DE WITT J Jr, *Indian Workers' Associations in Britain,* OUP/IRR Paperback, 1969
9 HEPPLE R, *Race, Jobs and the Law in Britain,* Allen Lane—The Penguin Press, 1968
10 INCOMES DATA SERVICES, *The New Race Law and Employment,* Handbook No 4, 1976
11 ILO, *Fighting Discrimination in Employment and Occupation,* International Labour Office, Geneva, 1968
12 JONES K and SMITH A D, *The Economic Impact of Commonwealth Immigration,* Cambridge University Press, 1970
13 KOHLER D, *The Employment of Black People in a London Borough,* CRC
14 METH M, *Brothers To All Men?* Runnymede Trust, 1972, *Here To Stay,* Runnymede Trust Industrial Unit, 1970

15 NICHOLSON B, *Racialism, Facism and the Trade Unions,* TGWU, 1974
16 PASCAL A, *Racial Discrimination in Economic Life,* Lexington Books, 1972
17 PEARN M A, *A Guide to the Race Relations Act 1976,* Industrial Society, 1976
18 REES T, *Policy or Drift?* Runnymede Trust Industrial Unit, 1971
19 RIMMER M, *Race and Industrial Conflict,* Heinemann, 1972
20 ROSE E J B *et al, Colour and Citizenship,* OUP/JRR, 1969
21 RUNNYMEDE TRUST, *Race and Jobs,* Runnymede Industrial Unit, 1971
22 SLATTER S St P & CRC, *The Employment of Non-English Speaking Workers; What Industry Must Do,* Community Relations Commission, 1974
23 SMITH D J, *Racial Disadvantage in Employment,* Political and Economic Planning, 1974, *The Facts of Racial Disadvantage,* Political and Economic Planning, 1976
24 STEWART M, *A Stitch In Time,* Runnymede Trust, 1973.

A fuller bibliography may be obtained from the Commission for Racial Equality. All the publications listed above as being published by the Community Relations Commission (CRC) and the Race Relations Board may also be obtained from the CRE.

APPENDIX 5

References

All the publications listed below as being produced by the Community Relations Commission (CRC) or the Race Relations Board may be obtained from the Commission for Racial Equality.

1 CRC, *Some People Will Believe Anything,* 1976
2 POWER J, *Western Europe's Migrant Workers,* Minority Rights Group, 1976
3 *Ibid*
4 CRC, *Op cit*
5 DANIEL W W, *Racial Discrimination in England,* Pelican, 1968, p57
6 *Ibid*
7 *Ibid,* p63
8 *Ibid*
9 SMITH D J, *Racial Disadvantage in Employment,* PEP, 1974
10 *Ibid,* p83
11 CRC, *Fact Sheet No 3, Employment,* p1
12 UNIT FOR MANPOWER STUDIES, *The Role of Immigrants in the Labour Market,* Department of Employment, 1977
13 SMITH, *op cit,* p89
14 HARGREAVES B J and PEACH L H, Social Responsibility: The Investment that Pays Off, *Personnel Management,* June 1976, Vol 8, No 6, pp20-25
15 *Ibid,* p21
16 *Ibid*
17 COMMISSION ON INDUSTRIAL RELATIONS, *Report No 76, Mansfield Hosiery Mills Ltd,* HMSO, 1974, p1
18 *Ibid,* p51
19 STEWART A and STEWART V, *The Management of Professionals.* Institute of Manpower Studies, 1974

20 INSTITUTE OF PERSONNEL MANAGEMENT, *Statement of Policy on Race Relations in Employment,* 1969, p1
21 DANIEL, *op cit,* p15
22 RACE RELATIONS BOARD, *Report of the Race Relations Board January 1975—June 1976,* HMSO, 1976, p12
23 RACE RELATIONS ACT 1976, Chapter 4, HMSO, 1976, p1
24 PEARN M A, *A Guide to the Race Relations Act 1976,* Industrial Society 1976, p3
25 *Ibid,* p8
26 RACE RELATIONS BOARD, Unpublished paper on *Changes in the Legislation on Racial Discrimination,* 1976, p1
27 PEARN, *op cit,* p23
28 RACE RELATIONS ACT 1976, *op cit,* p27
29 LONDON GRADUATE SCHOOL OF BUSINESS STUDIES, *Briefing Papers on the Trade Unions and Race Relations—The Race Relations Act 1976,* p5
30 INCOMES DATA SERVICES, *The New Race Law and Employment—Handbook No 4,* IDS, 1976, p69
31 *Ibid,* p64
32 RACE RELATIONS BOARD, *op cit*
33 SMITH D J, *The Facts of Racial Disadvantage,* PEP, 1976
34 *Ibid*
35 LEPPARD J W and KAUFMAN M, English for Asian Workers, *Industrial and Commercial Training,* September 1972
36 *Ibid,* p414
37 *Ibid,* p415
38 *Ibid,* p417
39 BANK OF CALIFORNIA, *Affirmative Action Programme*
40 Some questions taken from CRC, *Ethnic Minorities and Employment,* December 1975, No 1, p8
41 WAINWRIGHT D, *Race and Employment,* IPM, 1970, p25
42 INSTITUTE OF PERSONNEL MANAGEMENT, *op cit*
43 WAINWRIGHT, *op cit*
44 RACE RELATIONS BOARD, Fair Deal at Work, in *Equals,* October/November 1975, p3
45 *Ibid*
46 RACE RELATIONS BOARD, *Principles and Methods of Monitoring Equality of Opportunity in Employment,* 1975, p1
47 *Ibid*
48 *Ibid,* p2

Books from IPM

The IPM produces a large number of books on a wide range of management issues. Some of these are described below. For a free catalogue giving details of all our titles (over 85 now) write to the address on the title page. IPM books can be obtained through your local bookseller or direct from IPM.

Recruitment and Selection

P R Plumbley

Philip Plumbley has completely revised the original text of this book, but its purpose remains the same: to provide personnel specialists and line managers with a comprehensive and highly practical guide to all aspects of recruitment and selection. The author discusses in detail the approach to be used with candidates at every level from school leaver to junior manager.

"This is one of the few technical publications which I have been able to read like a novel and I became so engrossed that I found it impossible to put down until I reached the final page. It was disappointing to find that it had come to an end." *Works Management* 1974 214 pages

Finding Another Top Job

Bill Lubbock

This is a short, practical handbook dealing with the problems of the senior executive. The author points out that for such an executive, or anyone else with ambition who wants to change his job at senior level, conventional methods are often least likely to achieve success. The author explains the tactics of getting a top job and details his energetic, unorthodox approach which bypasses conventional methods. It embraces a totally planned, full time commitment entailing direct, thought-out approaches to target companies selected by research. The advice is based on the author's personal counselling experiences.

"All intelligent, provocative and no doubt effective stuff." *Birmingham Post* 1975 48 pages.

Developing Effective Managers

Tom Roberts

"The book offers a readable and comprehensive introduction for the thousands of managers who are approaching the subject for the first time and encourages the growing interest shown, particularly by small and medium sized companies, in the whole problem of management development and training." *Industrial Training International*

". . . . packs into 168 most readable pages, far more constructive ideas, lucid analysis and reasoned comment than many weightier volumes." *Technical Education* 1974 168 pages

Staff Appraisal

G A Randell, P M A Packard, R L Shaw and A J Slater

Since this book was first published the authors have been involved in running some 100 courses covering over 1500 managers and the principles described here are now being used in several large organizations, notably the Delta Metal Company, Beecham Pharmaceuticals and Cheshire County Council. This edition has been brought up to date by incorporating the authors' latest thinking.

". . . useful to those planning a performance appraisal training programme . . . written in a straightforward fashion and brings out some essential points of which any appraisal interviewer should have knowledge." *Personnel Psychology*

"a very useful book which would be of tremendous help not only to those who may be responsible for designing and implementing an appraisal scheme but to every manager anxious to improve his skill in staff appraisal." *Industrial Society* 1974 152 pages

Techniques and Developments in Management—a selection

Margaret Butteriss

In recent years a bewildering number of developments in management practices have taken place, and every manager needs to be aware of the implications of these changes for his organization. Margaret Butteriss examines new practices which are intended to enable the individual to achieve greater satisfaction from his work, such as job rotation and flexible working hours, as well as techniques and developments which are aimed at achieving corporate needs.

"An excellent guide for practitioners who, through lack of time or opportunity have been unable to keep ahead of the latest ideas in management. This book can be warmly recommended." *Times Educational Supplement* 1975 184 pages

Practical Manpower Planning

John Bramham

"(John Bramham) aimed for an easily readable book for the practising manager and personnel man and has succeeded." *British Gas Manpower Bulletin*

Contents: 1 The development of manpower planning. 2 The manpower planning process. 3 Identifying manpower requirements. 4 Analysing manpower supply I. 5 Analysing manpower supply II—wastage analysis. 6 Formulating manpower planning. 7 Manpower control, reporting and costs. 8 Information for manpower planning. 9 Computers and models in manpower planning. 10 Future developments in manpower planning. 1975 200 pages